FUNDAMENTAL CONCEPTS IN PHONOLOGY

Fundamental Concepts in Phonology
Sameness and Difference

Ken Lodge

Edinburgh University Press

© Ken Lodge, 2009

Edinburgh University Press Ltd
22 George Square, Edinburgh

www.euppublishing.com

Typeset in Adobe Sabon by
Servis Filmsetting Ltd, Stockport, Cheshire and
printed and bound in Great Britain by
CPI Antony Rowe, Chippenham and Eastbourne

A CIP record for this book is available from the British Library

ISBN 978 0 7486 2565 9 (hardback)

The right of Ken Lodge to be identified as author of this work has been
asserted in accordance with the Copyright, Designs and Patents Act 1988.

CONTENTS

PREFACE

This book is an attempt to bring together various strands of my work from over the past forty years, both as a researcher and as a teacher. The themes that I have chosen to discuss in some detail here can all be seen as problematical, even though typically they are taken for granted. My experience as a student, and then later as a researcher, taught me to question most things that were presented to me as accepted (and acceptable) dogma. This was the case despite being trained in an essentially structuralist tradition, before the appearance of *The sound pattern of English*, but I was also lucky enough to be introduced to the Firthian tradition of linguistics as an alternative viewpoint. The Chomskyan revolution, so-called, clearly was just that in the way language was approached as an object of academic investigation, but nevertheless it continued with many of the features of its predecessor, structuralism, especially in the area of phonology.

This book has thus grown out of a long dissatisfaction with the way in which many exponents of phonological theory do not approach their analyses in a consistent and principled way, often at a very basic level. It was quite striking that Goldsmith (1995a) (reviewed in Lodge, 1997) contained many such papers; these papers were claimed to be a selection of mainstream views on the structure of human phonologies. Lodge (1997) looks at a number of key issues which are fundamental to phonological theorizing, but which are treated as though they need not be revisited, despite several calls to that effect over the years. So, I am not so much concerned with whether the Obligatory Contour Principle, for example, is a valid and true statement of a linguistic universal as with whether the basic assumptions that lead to such a claim are valid. What can be said of academic monographs and anthologies can be said equally of intro-ductory textbooks in the field, so I will pay attention to the way issues are presented in some of these. This is particularly significant because today's students are tomorrow's phonologists.

In the process of developing my thoughts on phonological theory and analysis I have benefited from the teachings of others, from teaching others and from the many discussions I have had over the years with colleagues from the community of phonologists, not least at the many excellent annual Manchester Phonology Meetings and at the meetings of the Linguistics Association of Great Britain. There are too many friends and colleagues to mention individually, though there are several references to some of them in the text. However, I must pick out a few who have been particularly helpful in my project, even though they may not realize it. The order in which I list them is of no real significance, that is to say, help is not ordered, but its implementation usually is!

First of all, thanks to Sarah Edwards and her successor at Edinburgh University Press, Esmé Watson, for taking on this book in their catalogue, and for the subsequent help and encouragement to see it through to publication. After I met Dan Silverman I realized that there were scholars beyond the British Isles who shared at least some of my concerns, and his book (Silverman, 2006) has been an important inspiration. Equally my continued contact with those whom I might call the neo-Firthians, in particular, John Local and Richard Ogden, has made an important contribution to my work. Phil Carr has persisted in making me think what I mean by non-segmental; whether I have come up with a clear and suitable answer remains to be seen. My discussions with colleagues at the University of East Anglia have been mostly with people from schools of study other than my own: Diana Bell (mammalian biology), the late David Chadd (music), Roger Maskill and Roger Grinter (both chemistry) have all been very helpful to me with regard to their own fields of expertise and showed considerable interest in the general theme of sameness and difference. Bill Downes, who was in my School until his retirement, has always been engaging to talk to on any subject relating to language, and especially philosophical matters. My thanks to Tom Williamson, a colleague in the School of History, for allowing me the use of his scanner for the illustrations. So, thanks to everyone who has engaged in debate with me about linguistic matters, and, of course, to those whose language I have observed and analyzed over the years.

Ken Lodge
Norwich
January, 2009

1

THE NOTIONS OF SAMENESS AND DIFFERENCE

༄

Human beings classify the world around them. This classification occurs through language, which has led some linguists to go so far as to argue for linguistic determinism (Sapir, Whorf, Halliday). Whatever the merits and demerits of such a functional approach to the forms of language, as far as the human classification of the world (and beyond) is concerned, the development of a scientific account of reality has made the notions of sameness and difference central to such exploration. If x is considered 'the same as' y in certain respects, then x and y belong to the same category. If x is considered 'different' from y, then they belong to different categories. I want to consider these notions briefly in some other disciplines before going on to consider them and related concepts in the rest of the book within phonology.

I shall start, therefore, by taking a handful of instances to see the relevance of the arguments surrounding what counts as the same for areas outside linguistics and to see whether there are consistently applied criteria for helping the investigators to come to a conclusion about classification in any particular case. I will look at chemical formulae, aspects of mammalian biology, music and visual representation.

1.1 CHEMISTRY

Davenport & Hannahs (2005: 116) give an analogy from chemistry to elucidate the phonemic principle: they point out that the relationship between a phoneme and its allophones is like that between the chemical formula H_2O and the physical 'realizations' of a liquid, vapour or ice, each of which occur under specifiable conditions. This analogy is a good one because not only is the formulaic expression the abstraction from the actual occurrences, but the argument surrounding how much phonetics there is in a phonemic definition (see later Chapter 5) is paralleled by one in chemistry concerning the extent of the abstraction in the representation of formulae as H_2O, O_2, Cl_2, N_2, and so on. The physical nature and the chemical representation of entities in the world seem to be a clear indication of direct interpretation of the formulae in a way that is analogous to the intrinsic phonetic interpretation hypothesis (IPI; see, for instance, Carter, 2003, and Lodge, Local & Harlow, in prep.) in phonology, which is usually taken for granted by linguistics. However, the analogy breaks down in one vital respect: humans perceive the different physical states of H_2O and are conscious of the differences, hence the three separate lexical items *water, vapour, ice*, whereas allophones are not normally perceived by native speakers as phonetic variants but as phonologically the same thing.

Also, the chemical formulae are themselves used with different interpretations in different circumstances. As a default interpretation, H_2O represents a specific molecule of water. In (1.1) the emphasis is on an individual molecule of water formed from the reaction between one molecule of hydrogen and half a molecule of oxygen.

(1.1) $H_2 + \frac{1}{2}O_2 \rightarrow H_2O$

In (1.2), on the other hand, the representation refers to the fact that the reaction takes place in a mass of molecules, i.e. in solution in water.

(1.2) $NaCl \xrightarrow{H_2O} Na^+ + Cl^-$

So a chemical formula may refer to a generalized set of abstracted properties or a physical entity. This is entirely analogous to the use of the notion of the phoneme defined by phonetically based feature specifications in linguistics.

In chemistry there are also functional definitions. For instance, an acid can be defined as a substance which donates protons (H+), which may then neutralize hydroxide ions (OH^-) to form water (H_2O). However, acid may be shown as a formulaic expression, as in (1.3), analogous to (1.2), to indicate that a reaction only occurs in acid conditions.

(1.3) $A + B \xrightarrow{H^+} C + D$

In a further example, the chemical elements are classified in the periodic table by the properties of their atomic structures. Historically, the classification was based on both physical properties (atomic structure) and functional ones (their interactions with other elements).

The term 'property' is used to cover both of these aspects of element definition. In fact, both the physical and the functional properties of elements necessarily follow from atomic structures, but the periodic table was developed before this was understood.

The electron and its so-called wave/particle duality furnish yet another example of a functional definition. In certain circumstances an electron is a wave, and in others a particle. Common sense would suggest that an electron cannot be a particle and a wave, but this is not the best way to consider the problem. An electron is what it is and it is the conditions under which we observe it which change its apparent character. In some conditions an electron behaves as a wave, in others as a particle. The definition of an electron therefore depends on the circumstances in which we wish to understand it, and the way it functions in those circumstances. Considered as part of Newtonian mechanics the electron behaves as a particle; in its sub-nuclear state in the atom the electron is best considered to be a wave, the definition of which is a functional, mathematical one, a part of quantum mechanics.

Grinter (personal communication) has pointed out that in chemistry there is very little discussion of these issues along the lines in which I want to consider phonological features in the course of this book. Indeed, Grinter (2005) is a rare example of a topic introduced by a presentation of the historical context in which it is set, and an explanation of just what constitutes a theory.

1.2 BIOLOGY

I shall now consider the way in which animals are classified in biological terms paying particular attention to mammals and the phenomena milk, urine and fur. In any one species these items have different chemical and physical characteristics from the same items in other species. Why are these varied physical phenomena interpreted as 'the same'? In each case it is their respective function in the mammalian system: nourishment for the young, removal of liquid waste and provision of thermal insulation, camouflage and protection from radiation and injury. To a biologist it is not just the physical make-up but what each does in the life of the mammal that is important in this particular case, and the function is compared and classified across species. On the other hand, earlier (nineteenth-century) taxonomies were physically based on structural characteristics of each animal type. In the development of our understanding of what determines these structural patterns, genetic structure has taken over as the basis of classification. In this way it is easy to establish differences between what may seem superficially similar physical characteristics to the lay person; for example, rabbits and hares appear to be similar, and are classified within the same taxonomic order (Lagomorpha) and family (Leporidae) but in distinctive genera: *Oryctolagus* for the European rabbit and *Lepus* for the hares. Despite external physical similarities of long ears and back legs there are many differences. For example, one produces precocial (well-developed) young in a surface form and the other altricial young with no fur and closed eyes and ears, which remain in an underground nest for the first twenty-one days after birth. However, the answer in modern biology is a much more sophisticated physical one, namely genetic make-up: behaviour patterns and therefore functions of the mammal are determined by an interaction of the genetic material and the environment in which it lives. This gives us the functional interpretation of milk, urine and fur. (For an introductory discussion of mammals, see Macdonald, 2001.)

This has echoes of the notion that many linguists cling to, that [m] is always like an [m] in some unspecified sense (see Chapter 3 on biuniqueness), but which is easily demonstrated to be an untenable position. However, in phonology there is no such parallel to genetic precision, even though some linguists may indulge in wishful thinking and aim at determining physically based phonological universals (see Chapter 5 on phonetic implementation). Linguistics tries to draw a parallel relationship here between the phonetic raw material and the system of meaning distinctions in which that raw material functions. This relationship will be investigated in the rest of the book.

1.3 MUSIC

In music all instances of notes are physically different from all others, in much the same way as all instances of linguistic sounds are physically different, and yet some instances are classified as the same note while others are classified as different. The crucial criterion in this case is the rôle the instances play in the scale system being used. It is important to note, too, that 'the same note', that is, the same set of physical characteristics, can have a different rôle in different scale systems and that different scale systems recognize different intervals. Again, this is parallel to linguistic sounds having a different rôle in different phonological systems. Whereas there may be intellectually unconventional attempts to discard traditional systems of scales in modern music, the end result would be difficult to interpret without any kind of musical, as opposed to just physical, framework. In other words, music cannot function on a purely physical level any more than spoken language can.

A particular instance of sameness in music can be seen as having its parallels in language. It is often said that the same musical phrase or melody is used by the same or different composers in different pieces of music (for example, Tchaikovsky's use of the melody of the Russian National Hymn in *The 1812 Overture* and *Marche Slave*). Once again the question arises as to what 'the same' means here. It can only mean the tonal relationships between the sequenced notes, since other factors – for instance, the key in which the piece is written, the position in the piece, and the tempo – may well be different. In this case, from a functional point of view, within each piece of music the melodies have different functions, as they are in different musical environments. This is parallel to linguistic cases where observers may be tempted to say that English and German, for instance, have the same set of stop phonemes: /p t k b d g/. As pointed out clearly by Trubetzkoy (1939), this cannot be the case because the system-internal relationships are different, for example, the difference in the realizational behaviour of the voiced ones in codas.

One final point can be made with regard to notation: a sequence of notes can be made to look the same by writing them in conventional notation in the same way as the IPA symbols give the same impression to linguistic sounds. If the musical notation in Figure 1.1 appears in a number of musical scores, it will look the same wherever it appears; the stops of English and German can also be written with the same symbols, as above. It does not make them 'the same' in any meaningful and linguistically enlightening sense, any more than the sequence of notes is the same musically in different circumstances.

Figure 1.1   An example of conventional musical notation

For a general discussion of musical terms and concepts, see, for example, Sadie & Tyrrell (2001).

1.4 VISUAL REPRESENTATION

Finally, I want to consider the court figures on playing cards, as an instance of visual representation. I have chosen playing cards because (i) I have considerable knowledge of their nature and history (see, for instance, Lodge, [1991] 2003) and (ii) they offer a limited range of systematically related visual representations. 'The king of hearts', for instance, in a standard English pack, is represented by a man wearing a crown brandishing a sword behind his head in his left hand and holding the ermine edge of his cloak in the other. In Figure 1.2 I illustrate three modern versions of this figure. If we go back in time we can see more or less the same figure, but with feet instead of a double-headed representation, as in Figure 1.3 from the first half of the nineteenth century. To what extent are they 'the same'? In physical terms they have the characteristics I have just listed above. How, then, are the cards illustrated in Figure 1.4 also kings of hearts? Provided we have the corner indices 'K♥' it does not matter what pictorial devices are on the card itself. (This was not the case before the introduction of indices in the 1870s.) Figures 1.2 and 1.3 are examples of what is usually called the standard English pattern, whereas the central example in Figure 1.4 is the standard Paris pattern (with *R* as the index instead of *K*) and the others are non-standard cards. So despite their physical appearance all the illustrations are equivalent, and the card represented, the king of hearts, has the same value in bridge, poker or snap. Once again we see a functional definition of an item in a system.

In the case of playing cards it is interesting to note that historical

Figure 1.2   *Three modern versions of the king of hearts from standard English packs*

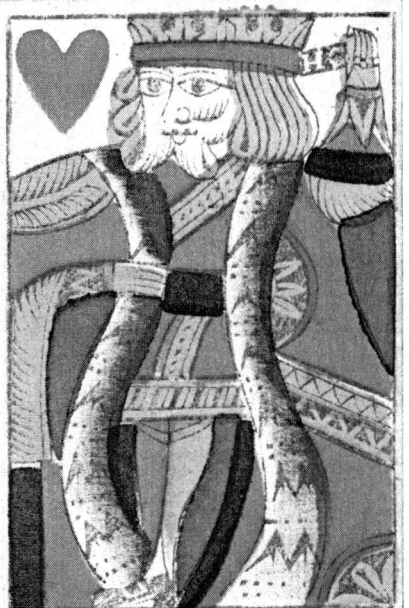

Figure 1.3 *Two standard English-pattern depictions of the king of hearts from the first half of the nineteenth century*

Figure 1.4 *The king of hearts from non-standard packs and (centre) the Paris pattern*

developments in their design have altered the need for distinctive representations. In the eighteenth century each figure of the English pack had distinct characteristics, such as those discussed in relation to the king of hearts. (Indeed, Alexander Pope, in *Rape of the Lock*, published in 1712, describes several court cards in some detail in a game of ombre, and the cards are easily recognizable from the descriptions even when no naming occurs: 'Th'embroidered king who shows but half his face' is the king of diamonds.) When corner indices were introduced in the nineteenth century to aid identification of cards in large hands – for example, thirteen cards in whist – the function of identification was taken over entirely by them. The simplest (and most boring!) pack would be four corner indices on each card and nothing else; the rest is, in fact, superfluous. It therefore no longer matters whether the king of hearts has two hands or whether the king of diamonds is in profile to the left.

1.5 OVERVIEW OF SAMENESS AND DIFFERENCE

In all instances of the use of the concepts 'sameness' and 'difference' there is a philosophical dimension, which also involves the notion of identity. The only absolute identity is token-identity of the individual; everything is identical with itself. To say that two non-identical entities are the same in some respect is to note a similarity between them in that respect. There are two forms of statement, strong and weak, that can be made with respect to such similarity: the strong is a sameness statement, as in (1.4), and the weaker a similarity statement, as in (1.5).

(1.4)   X is the same as Y with respect to characteristic P
(1.5)   X is like Y with respect to characteristic P

These could be equivalent if only one characteristic is involved. The greater the number of characteristics, the more differentiation of sameness is possible. The more characteristics that X and Y have in common, the more strongly they can be claimed to be the same in those respects; the fewer characteristics X and Y have in common, the more appropriate it is to talk of similarity between them as opposed to sameness. In addition, it is possible to add a contextual rider to either (1.4) or (1.5):

(1.4')   X is the same as Y with respect to characteristic P in all contexts
(1.4")   X is the same as Y with respect to characteristic P in some contexts
(1.5')   X is like Y with respect to characteristic P in all contexts
(1.5")   X is like Y with respect to characteristic P in some contexts

Some cases of sameness/similarity attributes define a type, where a set of individuals is perceived, inferred or stated truly to be the same with respect to P, or some set of P_{1-n}, which then form the criteria for the type. The set of individuals can differ in other respects, as long as they share P or P_{1-n} or, in some cases, some subset of P_{1-n}. This now gives us a number of possibilities for sameness and difference in the classification of types:

1. same with respect to a single property, a member of a type by virtue of a single, criterial property;
2. same with respect to a quorate subset of P_{1-n}, member of a type by virtue of some subset of a set of criterial properties;
3. same with respect to a set of properties P, member of a type by virtue of a set of necessary and sufficient criteria, all of which must be satisfied.

If we apply these to the example of playing-card figures discussed above, we can, in fact, come up with different but satisfying definitions of, say, the king of hearts in terms of physical characteristics for one particular standard pattern. By applying (3), we can define a standard English king of hearts as a male figure brandishing a sword behind his head, holding the ermine edge of his cloak and having a diagonal band of pattern across his chest (these are features that go back to the sixteenth century, though the band was originally a diagonal chain). By applying (2), we can include examples of standard English kings of hearts which may be missing one or more of these attributes, as in Figure 1.5, where the diagonal design or the king's

Figure 1.5 English-pattern kings of hearts

right hand is missing. If we applied (3) to such figures, we would have to refer to them as non-standard, or slightly deviant variants. If we apply (1), then, given the variety of representations referred to above, the criterion would have to be a functional one, that is, the place in the system of fifty-two cards that the king of hearts holds and his status in the various games that can be played with them.

Phonology is supposedly the link between 'reality' (the speech continuum) and the abstract system of the grammar. It, therefore, represents an area of debate in which the extent to which physical reality is part of the linguistic system has been a focal point for many years. If we want to know how 'same' and how 'different' sounds are, we need some very clear criteria for deciding. Of course, the term related to 'same' is 'similar', and that is the key to making decisions about phonological status: when are two similar utterances the same and when are they different? It is the purpose of the rest of this book to consider this issue in detail and investigate how consistent particular approaches to phonology are or have been with regard to specific instantiations of these basic principles of phonological analysis.

There has been an attempt recently to quantify sameness of sounds (Heggarty & McMahon, 2002) by using phonological features as the basis for comparison across related languages, for example, Romance or Germanic. However, given that this approach to the measurement of sameness works with phonological features that are based on the IPI hypothesis referred to above with little concern for phonetic minutiae, it is unclear how such a rationale brings us any nearer a proper understanding of what the best criteria are for judging sameness at this level. Of course, it must be remembered that in historical linguistics the notion of change interacts with notions of sameness; we have to be able to say, for instance, that *heart* and *Herz* are the same lexical item, and indeed that *hearty* and *cordial* are from the same root. The historical dimension I do not intend to pursue in this book, though it is relevant to the discussion of linguistic variation in Chapter 7.

1.6 A theoretical starting point

As a way of putting the critique that follows into a context, I now want to present an outline of a theory of phonology that takes all the issues on board. It is an approach that I have developed in the course of a number of publications, though not all issues are necessarily treated in each paper. For example, while the paper on assimilation

(Lodge, 1992) deals with feature layering, polysystemicity and under-specification it takes a segmental approach; on the other hand, the paper on German rhymal /r/ (Lodge, 2003a) attempts to bring all the issues together in the treatment of one phenomenon. It is also the case that the issues are not necessarily dependent on one another; for example, the issue of biuniqueness applies to any approach, whether segmental or not.

One crucial assumption that I make about phonological knowl-edge is that it is reflected in ordinary casual conversation. No privi-leged position is given to lexical entry forms, though that does not mean they have no rôle to play in phonology. The following further assumptions take account of the nature of spoken language, all of which will be discussed in the relevant chapters.

1. *Biuniqueness* – the identification of sounds in a linguistic system as the same must be based on the function of the sounds. For example, coda [s] and [z] are not to be identified with plural [s]/[z] because the latter function in a different way from the former, specifically, the latter alternate in the same morpheme, whereas the former distinguish meaningfully contrastive morphemes.
2. *Monosystemicity* – an a priori assumption that sounds in one syl-lable place are necessarily the same as those in another, largely on the tacit convention of sameness of letter-shape in a transcription, is unjustified. It is largely the adapted alphabetical transcriptions that encourage and underpin this view.
3. *Phonetic implementation* – the search for a universal set of pho-netic descriptors that can also be used for phonological analysis has clouded the issue of phonetic variability. While some kind of lowest common phonetic denominator of similar sounds may work in several cases there are plenty of other instances where it does not. The functional relatedness of quite dissimilar sounds is not unknown, for example, lenition congeners in Scots Gaelic, and the phonological relevance of acoustically dispersed characteris-tics is common, as in the sometimes foot-length realization of pho-nological elements such as /l/ and /r/ in many languages, and the very variable realizations of the so-called universal feature [ATR]. It follows that in many instances abstractness of phonological features with language-specific statements of implementation is necessary.
4. *Segmentation* – it is well known that real speech is not divided up into neat, segment-sized bits that are strung together like

beads on a necklace. Why then does the notion of the segment persist? Even the elaborate geometries developed since the mid-1980s cling to the notion of segment in having a sequence of anchoring sites and an attachment of phonetic features only at terminal nodes. The most obvious answer seems to be that linguists by their very training are literate, usually in some form of alphabetic writing. Despite the fact that it has been shown that alphabetic segmentation of speech does not develop naturally (see, for instance, Read et al., 1986) but is developed through learning to read and write, this evidence remains largely ignored. (One might ask, if segmentation skills are natural, why were the first writing systems non-alphabetic?) Given the adoption of the IPA alphabet (or equivalents) for the handy writing down of speech, it is easy to identify sameness through the letters used, rather than considering the phonetic facts and the functional rôles involved.

5. *One linguistic system* – at what level of social interaction is it appropriate to talk about 'language X'? Linguists describe 'English', 'German', 'French', but what are they actually doing? Very often they are describing a linguistic variety based on a standard written code, even when speech is supposedly the object of investigation. Of course, the many sociolinguistic investigations that have been undertaken specifically do not take this line, but it still leaves us with the question of whether we can legitimately speak of, for instance, 'the English language' as a meaningful concept. What language we speak in official terms is more often than not a matter of politics, social convention, history or religion, and maybe a combination of all of these; it is not usually a linguistic judgement.

6. *The relationship between sound and meaning* – since *The sound pattern of English* (SPE: Chomsky & Halle, 1968) approaches assuming some kind of derivation from an underlying (phonological) to a surface (phonetic) level have been pervasive. Since unconstrained derivation was criticized as too powerful, efforts to constrain the form of grammars have been attempted (see, for example, the discussions in Durand & Katamba, 1995 and Roca, 1997). The most constrained grammar will have no derivational mechanism, which includes deletion. If a grammar is to be truly declarative, it can entertain no change of phonetically interpretable features. To accommodate alternations, therefore, the phonological ('input') structures must be underspecified, so that the

alternating features can be supplied in the appropriate contexts (for a discussion of these issues, see Lodge, 2005).

To sum up, the phonology I envisage and argue for is a declarative, polysystemic, non-segmental one, which is associated with a particular linguistic variety in each case.

2

SAMENESS AND MEANINGFUL CONTRAST IN PHONOLOGY

༙

Similarity of sound is no safe guide to functional identity. (Firth, *Papers in Linguistics*)

I now want to turn to the specifically linguistic aspect of sameness and difference by looking first at a topic that all phonologists should agree with: the notion of meaningful contrast as the centre of phonological analysis. However, I would like to scrutinize it in a little more detail than is perhaps usual by considering how we, as phonologists, determine what constitutes sameness in phonology and what the consequences of that identification are. I will then elaborate on the topic in the later chapters of the book. As I have tried to show in the first chapter, one of the fascinating things about human beings is the way in which they classify: for the most part, sameness does not mean absolute identity, and sameness in one set of circumstances may be difference in others. To take a simple phonological example, native speakers of English typically identify regular plurality as being the same in all instances, despite the fact that phonetically we have [s], [z] and [ɪz] as predictable realizations; yet when distinguishing *mace* and *maze* native speakers have no difficulty in recognizing the same phonetic difference as marking a meaningful contrast. (Students of phonetics, even those who are quite competent in discrimination and transcription, typically transcribe regular plural forms with [s] even after voiced sounds, for example, [dɒgs], and the regular past tense as [d], even after voiceless sounds, for example, [wɔkd].) The significance of the reinforcement of such classifications by the system of English spelling will be discussed in Chapter 4.

Phonology is about differences of meaning signalled by sound. (I set aside consciously the growing literature on the phonology of sign language; this is not to underestimate its importance, but I wish to concentrate solely on the acoustic correlates of meaning in language. However, it is by no means obvious that the regularities of sign language should be described in the same terms as the phonology of spoken language.) It also has to do with sameness and identity. Sameness is the crux of the matter: what counts as the same, what counts as different? The answer to the latter part of the question relies on meaning, outside the strict domain of phonology. We ask the question: do *x* and *y* mean different things in language A? The first part of the question, however – that is, 'what is sameness?' – does not rely for its answer on external criteria, unless we see phonetics as external to phonology. The tension in phonology is always between the physical, phonetic sameness/similarity of individual occurrences in the speech continuum and the systematic, linguistic sameness determined by the structure of a particular language.

In order to explain the notion of meaningful contrast versus phonetic variability standard introductory textbooks (for example, Davenport & Hannahs, 2005; Gussenhoven & Jacobs, 2005) demonstrate complementary distribution as a criterion for allophonic status with examples similar to those in (2.1) from English. I have deliberately given more phonetic detail than is usual in order to be able to question the notion of phonetic sameness.

(2.1)   [pʰɪn]   [spɪn]   [nɪʔp̚]   [pʰeɪpə]
         [ˌbɪn]   [nɪb̚ˌ]   [neɪbə]

In the first vertical pair there is a difference of voice onset time: in *pin* voicing starts during the vocoid phase, in *bin* during the bilabial hold phase. This physical difference distinguishes two separate words, *pin* and *bin*. This difference is very important in English and is employed over and over again in combination with other articulations, too, for example, *tin* versus *din*, *cave* versus *gave*. In *nip* and *nib* we find a meaningful contrast carried by a different physical difference: glottal reinforcement versus cessation of voicing during the hold phase, both without release, or (not symbolized in (2.1)) voicelessness versus cessation of voicing during the hold phase, both with voiceless release; there is thus optional variation in the types of phonetic event that occur in these circumstances. In the intervocalic contoid phases of *paper* and *neighbour* there is yet another opposition, lack of vibration during the stop phase versus vibration. Such contrasts of meaning are sufficient to establish phonological relevance for the phonetic differences involved. All this is uncontentious.

But what of the differences in the examples on the same lines? They, too, are physically distinct from one another; delayed onset of voicing is clearly not the same as glottal reinforcement and lack of release. If we test for difference of meaning in the way in which we tested *pin* and *bin* and the other contrasts above, we end up with physical differences which are not meaningful. [pʰɪn] is not a different word from [pɪn] in English, and *[ʔpˀɪn] is physically impossible. In the case of the first two examples, either we say that [pɪn] 'doesn't occur in English' – a rash claim at best – or we say that it is a variant realization of *pin*. In fact, by an English native speaker it may be identified as *bin*, but the main point is that it is not a separate word from *pin* or *bin* in the English lexicon.

Having established meaningful distinctions of the various types above, all of which involve the activity of the vocal cords, at this point we have to ask about the status of the individual sound distinctions in the system. Is the difference between *pin* and *bin* the same as that between *nip* and *nib*? Of course, our spelling system with the Roman alphabet suggests that it is, and this is reinforced by the choice of IPA symbols used to represent the sounds. (In Chapter 4 I shall discuss the work of Morais and his associates on literacy and segmentation and the effect of alphabetic writing on our perception of sounds.) Certainly, both distinctions involve bilabial closure and a difference of phonation, but a different difference in each case. But this is where we turn to our knowledge of phonetics to try to answer the question. Our concern with sameness is now of a different order: a matter of physical attributes not meaning. The danger is (and I shall return to this in a consideration of abstractness in Chapter 5) that if we have no criteria other than distribution on which to base our judgements, then the non-distinctive [pʰ] can be identified with [t] intervocalically and [ŋ] in final position, with which it does not contrast meaningfully, that is, they are all in complementary distribution. It was for this reason that the structuralists (for example, Hockett, 1955: 156–8) introduced the criterion of phonetic similarity for realizations of the same phoneme, so that, for instance, initial [h] and final [ŋ] in English cannot be classified as the same on the grounds of complementary distribution alone. (See also the discussion in Clark & Yallop, 1995: 97–8.)

So, the question is: on what grounds do we classify the different bilabial articulations in English which are in complementary distribution? In terms of the data I have presented here (which is by no means exhaustive, even for one variety of English) it is inaccurate to say that the distinction is one of voicelessness versus voice, so that any combination of bilabiality and voicelessness can be identified as the same, because in final position we often have glottal reinforcement not voicelessness. Of course, we can say that the combination of voice and bilabiality (without nasality) is in contrast with the combination of bilabiality with other phonation types, so that the contrast can be defined in terms of presence or absence of vibration of the vocal cords. Note that in a system of binary features [+voice] can mean 'having vibrating vocal cords' and [−voice] can mean 'not having vibrating vocal cords'. The latter would then need to be further differentiated as to whether the sound had open or closed vocal cords. Very often, however, the interpretation of [−voice] is taken to mean 'having open vocal cords', that is, a positive definition, with no further consideration of vocal cord position. For instance, in Gussenhoven & Jacobs (2005: 63) and Odden (2005: 146–7) the different states of the glottis are covered by three binary features: [voice], [spread glottis] and [constricted glottis]. The analysis of phonation types in this way can lead to contradictory specifications of the English stops. Gussenhoven & Jacobs (2005: 78) represent English onset /p/ (in *pens*) as [−voice], [−spread], [−constr]. Since in English aspiration is not contrastive, it has to be derived from [-voice] in onset position (see, for example, Kahn, 1976, and Selkirk, 1982). But aspirated stops are [+spread] (Gussenhoven & Jacobs, 2005: 63), so a feature change is necessary. Odden (2005: 148–9) picks up this particular point in relation to English /p t k/, and concludes that [−spread] is the 'underlying value'. This already points up issues of the universality of distinctive features and monosystemicity that I will address in later chapters. Because phonetically based phonological features are used to define phonological contrasts in all languages, there is a tension between those contrasts and the phonetics used to realize them; further, an insistence on one definition covering all phonological environments produces more such tensions. In the same way that onset voiceless stops in English will require a change from [−spread] to [+spread], the realizations of the 'same' coda stops, as illustrated in (2.1), will have to have their specification of [constr] changed from minus to plus. So, onset [−voice], [+spread], [−constr] and coda [−voice], [−spread], [+constr] are both represented as [−voice], [−spread], [−constr] in the underlying form because of the notion of meaningful contrast. We can also see that such an assumption of phonetically based phonological features forces a derivational account of the relationship between the lexical forms and their realizations.

As a way of avoiding such cumbersome solutions to the difference between underlying and surface structure, Government Phonology (GP, for example, Harris, 1994 and Harris & Lindsey, 1995) proposes elements of phonological structure that are directly interpretable as phonetic events. For the purposes of representing phonation there are two elements: slack vocal cords (**L**) and stiff vocal cords (**H**). Unaspirated voiceless stops and stops with little voicing before release have neither element (neutral). So English onset stops are specified as **H** (/p t k/) or neutral (/b d g/). Aspiration is the particular phonetic interpretation of **H** in single-onset position. In codas where glottal stops and glottally reinforced realizations occur, GP uses licensing conditions and government relations, a presentation of which goes beyond the scope of the present discussion. Basically, the combination of the stop element (**ʔ**), the coronal place element (**R**) and **H**, which are found in onset position is simplified under specific licensing conditions by suppressing the phonetic realization, by means of delinking, of either the element **H** (or its associated element **h**, noise, typically associated with fricatives and the release phase of stops; see Harris, 1994: 123), or both **H** and **R**. The former results in the glottally reinforced coronal, the latter in the glottal stop. Note, however, that glottal closure is not classified together with the elements of phonation in this analysis, and both **H** and **h** represent aspiration.

In the case of *spin* and *paper* in (2.1) I have used the same symbol for both the onset [p] in the first example and the intervocalic [p] in the second. On this basis, it is easy to say that these two realizations are the same, that is, they are both unaspirated. Is this, however, an accurate statement at either the phonetic or the phonological level? The answer has to be no to both. Firstly, phonetically there may be variable amounts of aspiration in the case of post-nuclear intervocalic voiceless stops in English, but not in those following /s/. From a realizational point of view the intervocalic /p/ is also susceptible to lenition in many varieties, that is, we may find [peɪɸə] as a realization; this does not occur after /s/. Furthermore, there is a contrast between intervocalic /p/ and /b/, but no such contrast after /s/. So from a functional point of view, the behaviour of post-/s/ onset /p/ is different from that of post-nuclear intervocalic /p/. Again it depends on the amount of detail we, as phonologists, wish to recognize. If this detail is a matter of observational regularities, then it should be part of the phonological statements of a language.

In many simple cases like this a reliance on a careful 'factoring out' of the phonetic features involved will give the desired results, namely that the examples on the top row of (2.1) all contain realizations of the same phoneme, /p/, and the bottom row contains realizations of /b/. But what about cases where the common denominators are more difficult, if not impossible to determine? In (2.2) we have examples from a different variety of English from those in (2.1).

(2.2)　[tʰen] *ten*　[leʔə] *letter*　[neʔ] *net*

Such alveolar and glottal realizations are analyzed as being allophones of the phoneme /t/ (cf. Wells, 1982, Lodge, 1984, Harris, 1994). In cases such as this there are hardly any common denominators, though both realizations are stops, one oral, one glottal. Phonetic similarity is not much of a criterion to help us here. Certainly, there are some varieties of English in which a different criterion can be invoked; in those accents where [neʔ] has derived forms [netɪn] *netting* and [netɪd] *netted*, then there is a morphological criterion to guide our analysis. But if the derived forms are [neʔɪn] and [neʔɪd], then morphology is no help either.

We can discuss the issue of morphological alternations and their importance to phonology by first of all taking the straightforward kind of phenomenon, such as English regular plurals and morpheme-final obstruents in German. The former I have already mentioned briefly at the beginning of this chapter. The question that I shall consider in the next chapter is: to what extent should we identify plural marker [s] with, say, the [s] in *sue* or *mace*, or the plural marker [z] with the [z] of *zoo* or *maze*? The German case I shall consider in later chapters. Again it is a question of identification: are the voiceless/voiced obstruent alternations in *blieb/blieben*, *Rad/Rades*, *Krieg/Krieges*, *brav/braver*, *las/lasen*, respectively in word-final and word-internal positions, to be related to the separate contrasting phonological entities in *Pass/Bass*, *Leiter/leider* and so on?

There are even more unusual, non-phonetic relationships, such as [t] and [ɣ] in Scots Gaelic, as the base and lenited forms, respectively, of what can be interpreted as the same phonological entity (see also later chapters for further discussion of lenition in Scots Gaelic). In this case it has to be the morphosyntax of the language that determines the association of two very different articulations. There are a number of morphosyntactic triggers of lenition: genitive, adjectival intensifiers, the definite article and past tense, as in the examples in (2.3).

(2.3)　[vẽə̃ntən] of mountains　[pẽə̃ntən] mountains
　　　　[kleː xɔrəx] very steep　[kʰɔrəx] steep
　　　　[ə xɬax] the stone　[kʰɬax] stone
　　　　[xɔʃiç mi] I walked　[kʰɔʃiç] walk

(Some of these examples are from recordings of Skye Gaelic; this accounts for vowel differences in particular *vis-à-vis* published treatments. Other examples are from Dilworth & Macleod, n.d. For further detailed discussion, see MacAulay (1992: 238–47) and Gillies (1993: 166–71), who both treat the phenomenon in terms of morphophonemics; Russell (1995: 231–57) also gives a historical overview for the Celtic languages in general.) Some of the alternations that are exhibited are given in (2.4) with others added.

(2.4)   Radical consonant: [pʰ tʰ kʰ p t k m f s]
         Lenited equivalent: [f h x v ɣ ɣ v Ø h]

Some of these relationships can be seen as phonetically based, for example, stop: fricative, in line with the traditional view of lenition, but, clearly, the coronals do not follow the pattern. [tʰ] and [h] ([x] in some dialects) alternate and so do [t] and [ɣ], as in [tʰeriʃ] *tairis* 'kind, loving', [heriʃ] *thairis* in post-nominal attributive position; and [tuːlan] *dùbhlan* 'defiance, challenge', [a ɣuːlan] *a dhùbhlan* 'to the quick'. In this case it is the functional relationship of morphologically determined alternating realizations that establishes the phonological pairing of phonetically dissimilar sounds.

So there are three levels on which we need to consider sameness and difference: (1) the phonetic, (2) the phonemic, (3) the systemic. We have discussed the phonetic level in relation to allophonic distribution and will need to consider it further under the heading of biuniqueness (Chapter 3). Phonemic sameness leads to a consideration of abstractness and the relationship between phonetics and phonology (Chapter 5). Systemic sameness is concerned with the extent to which contrastive systems are the same throughout the language; for instance, we have to address the question of whether the system of onset contrasts should be assumed to be the same as the system of coda contrasts in the same language. This leads us to a consideration of monosystemicity (Chapter 3). Silverman (2006) removes the issue of phonetic similarity from instances of simple complementary distribution by claiming that only alternating forms can be legitimately considered as variants of the same phonological entity. Two quotations from his work sum up his position: 'articulatory or acoustic similarity among sounds is neither a prerequisite, nor a diagnostic, for allophonic relatedness' (Silverman 2006: 87); 'the maintenance of meaning upon alternation is both necessary and sufficient for learners to determine allophonic relatedness' (ibid.: 93). Odden (2005: 46) points out that there are indeed alternations involving aspirated and unaspirated stops in American English, which apply in British English, too, and include glottally reinforced variants, as in (2.5).

(2.5)   [ɡɹanʔtˑ] *grant*   [ɡɹantə] *granter*   [ɡɹantʰɹi] *grantee*

So there is evidence that at least some instances of the distribution of stops in English are morphologically motivated, but we still need to consider whether the non-alternating instances, for example, *cant*, *banter*, *guarantee*, are identified as tokens of the same phonological unit in all cases (see further, Chapter 3).

The issue of what constitutes the data for phonological theorizing and the nature of the output of the grammar also needs consideration. Typically, the material to be studied is presented in most phonology books and articles as sets of phonetic transcriptions using the IPA alphabet or some American alternative. What is usually not acknowledged is that such transcriptions are already processed in some way to make them ready for an appropriate analysis. So, textbooks give data as in (2.1) in which the identification of the different variants of /p/ and /b/ is made easy and obvious by the choice of letter with or without diacritics. However, even (2.1) is more detailed than in some presentations, for example, Davenport & Hannahs (2005: 114–15); Carr (1999: 37), though some phonetic detail is given in the transcriptions; Odden (2005: 44–6). Phonemic contrasts may even be established on the basis of phonemic symbols: [pɪn] versus [bɪn], [tɪn] versus [dɪn], and so on, or even using orthographic forms, for instance, Gimson (1962: 45) and Giegerich (1992: 34), with the phonetic detail coming later. And, whereas allophonic details such as in the top row of (2.1) are given as data in descriptions of allophonic variants, transcriptions such as [ˌbɪn] and [nɪbˑ] do not appear. Presumably, the details of voice onset and offset time and whether stops are released or not are considered to be low-level phonetic effects that can somehow be ignored. Such an approach certainly makes the issue of sameness and difference less difficult; 's' is the same as 's', 'p' the same as 'p', anyone can see that. This is one of the aspects of phonological representation that is not discussed much explicitly but is implicit in any visual representation of speech (one symbol per phoneme or per phone), namely that sameness is often based on the symbolic representation, as opposed to the nature, of the sounds themselves. Indeed, it is possible to analyze similarities and differences in representations that purport to be phonetic without knowing what they are supposed to represent. (See also Archangeli & Pulleyblank's warning about transcriptions (1994: 159–61).)

Of course, it could be argued that in introductory textbooks it is necessary not to overwhelm the student with too much detail in the first instance, so that particular points can be made simply and one at a time. This is a very reasonable pedagogical point, but what we need to know is when does the detail come into the picture? The answer is that it usually never does. Once the data have been set up and presented in such a way that our analyses work nicely, there is never any need to muddy the waters with the phonetic detail. The analyst controls the presentation of any details that are necessary for the analytical outcome; it would be up to other analysts to provide their own contradictory data by way of refutation. There are few books like Kelly & Local (1989) in which narrow transcriptions are given as a basis for discussion. (For a similar discussion of the data and aims of phonology from the point of view of sociolinguistic variation, see Docherty & Foulkes, 2000.) The dominant view of what constitutes data for analysis means that many aspects of phonology are left unquestioned and inherited from one analysis to another. This is particularly the case with 'library phonology', the use of previous analyses to exemplify or refute particular points of theory. This reliance on (at least) second-hand material as the sole basis of analysis takes the discussion further and further away from the facts of native-speaker production. There is usually some 'field phonology' at the beginning of the chain of borrowing the material, but sometimes this, too, is already handily parcelled up into phoneme-like examples. Take, for instance, the basic material of the *Survey of English Dialects* (Orton et al., 1962–71). In the published material there is a striking lack of instances of a labiodental nasal [ɱ], even though there are questions prompting the answers *seven* (VII.1.6) and *eleven* (VII.1.9), for instance. This should strike anyone who knows the realizations of colloquial English as suspicious, but, of course, from a historical perspective, which is the main stimulus of the survey, [ɱ] has nothing but allophonic status, so is therefore presumably deemed uninteresting. But given this, what are we to make of some of the other impressionistic transcriptions in the survey, many from unrecorded speech? Another example of reliance on old fieldwork for phonological analysis is that of [ATR] harmony in Tugen (Kalenjin), which I will discuss in more detail in later chapters, discussed in Local & Lodge (1996 and 2004) and Lodge, Local & Harlow (in prep.). In this case there is also an apparent determination to ignore or misinterpret the earlier acoustic and articulatory investigations of the feature related to tongue root position (for example, Lindau, 1975, 1978 and Lindau Jacobson & Ladefoged, 1973).

A more sophisticated presentation of phonological sameness and difference relies on feature specifications rather than letter-symbols. Carr (1993a), for instance, gives many feature matrices throughout the discussion of various languages, so that it is clear what the symbols actually stand for. If two feature arrays are the same, then the sounds they represent are also the same. An approach of this sort, referred to briefly in Chapter 1, is taken by Heggarty (2000) and Heggarty & McMahon (2002) in a research project to try to quantify sameness in phonology in the context of historical development. Degrees of similarity can be measured by counting the number of features in as many arrays as are appropriate. They demonstrate the technique by using Romance languages and comparing, for instance, the similarities between modern reflexes of Vulgar Latin *caballu* 'horse'. But this measure of similarity presupposes a segmental theory of phonological structure with fully specified binary features with a direct phonetic interpretation. This is certainly the approach taken by Kessler (2005), who discusses what he refers to as phonetic comparison algorithms, but is clearly focused on the phonological features of segments; he also refers to the 'phonetic inventory' (2005: 248). So, the phonological feature array represents the phonetic characteristics to be compared. But this does not help us compare real phonetic events, which are not necessarily representable in binary or segmental terms (see further, Chapters 4 and 5 and Docherty & Foulkes, 2000).

Any criteria of sameness at the physical level that ignore the functional aspect of the linguistic system will at best involve a complex set of morphophonemic statements to account for the relationships of alternating forms. That is to say that if we insist that the plural morpheme in English has the separate phonemic forms /s/, /z/ and /ɪz/, then we will have to invoke morphophonemic rules to relate what would otherwise be separate entities in the system. I shall return to this in Chapter 3. Physical similarity versus functional identity is discussed in Silverman (2006: 95–100), referring to Shepard, Hovland & Jenkins (1961), who investigated visual categorization. Silverman argues that their investigations of vision show up similarities with linguistic classification. Physical similarity as a categorization criterion is easier to use in learning than non-similarity, but if the latter is associated with functional similarity, then the initial difficulties of category learning based on non-similar characteristics are soon overcome. Since the experiments were carried out on visual images, we can see the relevance of the functional criterion to our earlier instance of playing-card court figures discussed in Chapter 1. Whereas it may be dangerous to assume too close a parallelism between visual and linguistic categorization (cf. Silverman's caution in this respect (2006: 100)), irregular (that is, non-phonetic) classifications in language also appear to require extra effort to learn. For instance, the results of the Great Vowel Shift in modern English are sets of related forms with a tenuous phonetic basis. (This did not prevent Chomsky & Halle, 1968 from making the phonetics fit the paired vowels; see further discussion below in Chapter 5.) Since the vocabulary is learnèd and for some people rare, speakers of modern English have two alternatives: to use the non-phonetic relationships, as in *opaque–opacity*, usually learned from the standard written form of the language, or use the 'easier', productive way of signalling the relationship, as in *opaque–opaqueness*. (See also the discussions of these relationships and their acquisition in Aronoff & Schvaneveldt, 1978, Jaeger, 1986, and Wang & Derwing, 1986.) One final example of the difficulty of non-phonetic categories being more difficult to learn is that furnished by the acquisition of Irish initial mutations by non-native speakers in the Irish educational system. Despite their grammatical function, the consonantal alternations, such as those referred to above in Scots Gaelic, prove to be consistently problematical to acquire for English-speaking Irish, who have to learn the language at school. (See Kingsley O'Hagan & Krämer, 2004 for details; see also Dorian, 1977 on lenition loss in Scots Gaelic.)

Rather than starting from the phonological analysis with which the observer wishes to end up and explaining away phonetic detail as predictable (and even irrelevant), what I am suggesting here is the paying of closer attention to phonetic detail as the basis of any analysis and a scrutiny of the consequences of the basic a priori assumptions made about phonology, which are often invoked without discussion. Such considerations will constitute the themes of the following chapters.

3

BIUNIQUENESS AND MONOSYSTEMICITY

∾

Biuniqueness. Any phone in a given environment must be an allophone of one and only one phoneme – to prevent ambiguity and secure unique read-off. (Lass, *Phonology*)

3.1 INTRODUCTION

In this chapter I want to consider analyses which seem to assume some kind of biuniqueness. Thereby I want to demonstrate the way in which biuniqueness, and with it monosystemicity, obscure the facts and complicate the phonological analysis of language.

Fudge (1967) discusses abstractness in phonological primes, an issue I return to in Chapter 5. In this paper he argues that the most important reason for distinguishing between phonetics and phonology is what Chomsky (1964) calls biuniqueness. The argument was originally made against a background of structuralist phonemics which equated the two. Any speech sound is interpreted as a segment and classified with a universal set of descriptive articulatory labels. This process of interpretation classifies the sounds as segments of the same type (phones): stops, fricatives, front vowels, nasals etc. Once such an identification is made it is fixed for the language in question and all similarly identifiable segments are associated with that class. Thus, in English, onset [d] and coda [d] are identified as being the same on all occasions; the same applies to onset [b] and coda [b], onset [m] and coda [m], and so on. Phonetic differences – for example, delayed onset of voicing in the onset position, pre-release cessation of voicing in the coda – are ignored. This fixing of the phonetic descriptions of sound segments on a once-and-for-all basis occurs before the fixing of the phonemic contrasts. The contrasts are established in the usual way, on the basis of difference of meaning, and also on the basis of the phonetic similarity of the phones under investigation. Once a set of distinctive features has been established as the basis of a phonemic definition, for instance /m/ as a bilabial nasal, then all occurrences of the combination of bilabial and nasal are associated exclusively with that phoneme. Thus, in English both occurrences of bilabial + nasal in the assimilated form [tem men] *ten men* are associated with the phoneme /m/ (cf. Gimson, 1962: 270–1). A word like *ten* would have three phonemic forms: /tem/, /ten/, /teŋ/ and the one ending in /n/ would have the allophonic variants [teɱ] and [teṇ] besides [ten], presumably because there are no separate labiodental and dental nasal phonemes in English. All these forms are the product of assimilation of place before obstruents and nasals. Structuralist phonemicists were not concerned with native speaker knowledge, so there seemed to be no problem with one word having three different phonemic forms, since they were not forms stored in anyone's mental lexicon. Chomsky (1964) demonstrated that if phonemic forms of words and morphemes are psychologically real for native speakers, then they represent the stored knowledge about each distinct lexical item in the language, and it makes no sense to allow some items to have three distinct forms. Even within a structuralist approach, if phonemes carry distinctions of meaning, then it is still inconsistent to assume one word can have distinctive alternate forms predictable by context, unless one is prepared to extend the morphophonemic level to absurdity, covering all assimilations such as those of English /n/. The alternative is for lexical items to have one distinct form in the lexicon representing the many predictable phonetic variants. For this to be the case, the exclusive association of phonemic and phonetic forms (biuniqueness) must be abandoned. The practical result of this is that occurrences of (similar) constellations of phonetic features do not have to be identified as 'the same'. This applies at both the phonetic and the phonemic level. So, to return to our English example, /n/ has the positional variants [m, ɱ, ṇ, n, ŋ], as exemplified by the assimilated forms of *ten*, despite the fact that English has the phonemes /m/ and /ŋ/. There is no longer a problem with the claim that the first [m] in [tem men] is an allophone of /n/ whereas the second one is an allophone of /m/.

Despite Chomsky's intervention, the principle of biuniqueness seems still to be assumed in many analyses and is the implicit support of a monosystemic approach to phonology. This is true even of Chomsky & Halle (1968). Although determining that all cases, even those such as *sane/sanity* etc., have single underlying forms removes morphophonemics from the grammar, establishing, as a consequence, such rules as Trisyllabic Laxing, the free-ride principles encourages the phonologist to identify the vowel in, say, *wane*, with the vowel in *sane*, despite the fact the former is not subject to any alterations, and thus trades on the notion of biuniqueness. In many cases we shall see that the level of morphophonemics is needed only because of phoneme identification. It is interesting to note that Chomsky & Halle (1968: 11 and refs) specifically rule out this level as a mediation between morphemes and phonemes, themselves elements on two separate levels. The position they take leads them to the Unique Underlier Condition (the term comes from Lass, 1984: 63), which requires only one lexical form for any (non-suppletive) morpheme (Chomsky & Halle, 1968: 12), a requirement explicitly made by Sprigg (1957) in the polysystemic approach of Firthian prosodic analysis. (See further below.)

3.2 MORPHOPHONEMIC ALTERNATIONS

There is a crucial issue that relates to the status that we give to the notion of meaningful distinction, whether at the morphological or the phonological level, and how and where we deal with morphophonemic alternations. (For a long discussion of morphophonemic alternations, see Lass, 1984.) Again it's an issue of sameness.

In discussing the morphophonemic alternations of voice in *twelve/twelfth* and *dogs/cats*, as opposed to positionally determined allophonic variation, such as aspiration in English, Mohanan (1995: 33) claims that the former type of alternation 'is clearly phonemic, because in English, *f* and *s* contrast with *v* and *z* respectively'. He also classifies as this type of alternation the optional assimilation of [hɔrs] in *horseshoe* [hɔršsuu] (Mohanan's transcriptions). What is the important criterion for him in distinguishing between phonemes? Surely, it is difference of meaning ('contrast'). But in the case of the morpheme *twelv/f* and the plural morpheme in English there is *no* contrast, the variant realizations mean the same thing in each case and are entirely predictable. So Mohanan relies on biuniqueness in the same way Gimson (1962) does. In the case of *horseshoe* the same argument would apply, if we accepted that the two occurrences of [š] were reliably identifiable as the same. Some speakers may round the lips for both occurrences; others, on the other hand, have lip-rounding only for the second fricative, in which case identity is even more questionable. A simple solution in the latter case is that the palato-alveolar fricative, whether rounded or not, is an allophone of /s/ before palatal and palato-alveolar phonemes. (For a detailed discussion of [s]–[ʃ] assimilation, see Nolan, Holst & Kühnert, 1996.)

The phonetic difference of assimilated articulations would also apply in the case of English /n/, discussed above, where many speakers combine gestures in the direction of the alveolar ridge with the other place of articulation. (See Barry, 1985; Kerswill, 1985; Wright, 1986; Nolan, 1992 and Local, 1992 for details.)

In the light of the observed phonetic details of assimilated forms it is crucial that we have a set of clear criteria for determining what is important phonologically in that phonetic detail and what is not. It is certainly inadequate to ignore it as trivia of performance; either phonology is abstract and not driven by the phonetic detail at all or the detail gives us insights into how the phonology works. (See also Ogden's discussion of the relevance of phonetic detail to phonological analysis, 1997, 1999; also Scobbie 2005a, 2005b.) Of course, the whole issue is complicated by the assumption of segmentally identifiable phones as the raw phonetic data to be analyzed and a close association of phonological and phonetic features. This is an issue that will be discussed more fully in Chapter 5, but it often means that the phonology drives the phonetics. As we saw in the previous chapter, articulatory features have been chosen in order to define what is usually termed a natural class, such that [p pʰ ˀp], for instance, are all classified as voiceless, bilabial stops, and this is despite the fact that the last one is glottally reinforced, a characteristic produced by the completely opposite position of the vocal cords, namely closed, as opposed to an open position for the production of voicelessness. It would seem that the desired phonological answer, namely that in a language like English these stops are to be classified as the same, drives the choice of criterial features at the phonetic level. Expressed differently, complete bilabial closure with no accompanying vibration of the vocal cords might be a more suitable formulation. It is important to note that 'sameness' in this context is giving way to the related notion of 'similarity' that we discussed in Chapter 1.

I would now like to take a particular instance of morphophonemic analysis, which was referred to briefly in Chapter 2, where phone identification on the basis of phonetic similarity is of no help at all in understanding the grammatical system of the language in question. Ternes (1989) presents a phonemic analysis of Scots Gaelic. The grammatical relevance of the alternating word-initial consonants of nouns, adjectives and verbs in all the Celtic languages is well-known (cf. Ball, 1993), but it causes phonemic analyses a great deal of trouble. For example, Ternes (1989: 13) follows Dorian's (1965: 80) arguments relating to [f], which occurs as a result of initial mutation (the traditional term for the alternations) as well as word-initially in base forms. He quotes Dorian: 'Obviously the phone [f] remains objectively the same whether it occurs in a base form or in a secondary form, and this fact must be preserved in any statement of the phonology of the dialect.' Biuniqueness writ large! And the same argument as that used by Mohanan (1995) discussed above. Ternes agrees wholeheartedly with this position, and goes on to establish [b d g], all products of nasal mutation, as separate phonemes, even though there are no minimal pairs, except between different morphological forms of the same lexical item. So, he gives the 'contrasts' in (3.1) as evidence of a kind of parallelism.

(3.1)　[ha pʰɛ̃n]　'There's a pen . . .'
　　　　[ha pɛ̃n]　'There's a woman . . .'
　　　　[ha bɛ̃n]　'The pen is . . .'
　　　　[ha vɛ̃n]　'The woman is . . .'

(He gives an alternative with initial [bʰ] for [bɛ̃n], which is only found in conservative speakers in the Applecross dialect he is describing.) The argument goes: since [pʰ] and [p] contrast and are separate phonemes, then [b] and [v] must be separate phonemes because they contrast. But the same point applies here as in the case of German final obstruents to be discussed below and in the later chapters: [pʰ] and [b] alternate in the same morpheme, just like [p] and [v]. He even makes the point that Celtic initial mutations are very like German umlaut (Ternes, 1989: 15–16) because there are non-alternating versions of [y ʏ ø œ]. Quite so, but an insistence on the identity of these phones, and with it a monosystemic approach, are an unwarranted straightjacket. (For analyses of German umlaut that do not identify alternating and non-alternating forms, see Lodge, 1989 and Wiese, 1996.)

The radical and (non-nasal) lenition forms for the stops, fricatives and /m/ are as in (3.2) (repeated from (2.4)).

(3.2)　Radical consonant:　[pʰ tʰ kʰ p t k m f s]
　　　　Lenited equivalent:　[f h x v ɣ ɣ v Ø h]

where Ø = zero. This is the 'standard', mainland version of some of the relationships; in the Islands some of the realizations are different, for example, lenited /tʰ/ and /s/ are often [x]. Other consonants, too, are involved in lenition and so-called nasalization. (Further details are given in Ternes, 1989, MacAulay, 1992, Gillies, 1993 and Russell, 1995.) However, the examples in (3.2) are sufficient for my purposes.

In addition there are a few assimilated forms as well; for instance, *fàsmhor* 'growing' from *fàs* 'increasing' + *mór* 'big' is [fɑːsfəɹ] with initial radical (lexical) [f] and internally lenited /m/ without voice because of the preceding [s]. This gives us three instances of [f]: radical, lenited and assimilated lenited of different radical consonants. What reason is there for identifying these as the same? The relationship between radical [pʰ] and its lenited equivalent [f] is more important in the statement of the systematic regularities of Scots Gaelic than any presumed a priori phonetic identity of radical [f] and lenited [f]. The same applies to radical [m] and its lenited equivalent with assimilation to a preceding [s]: [f]. With regard to the voiced stops the argument is slightly different. There are no distinctive voiced stops for them to be associated with, except word-internally in loanwords and after homorganic nasals. Voice is not distinctive in radical [pʰ] versus radical [p]; it can, therefore, be left unspecified in their lexical definitions. Voice occurs only in the case of the noun being definite. The manner of articulation is not distinctive either, because there is an alternation between stop and fricative realizations. (For a discussion of underspecification and non-destructive phonology, and a more detailed analysis of the consonants of Scots Gaelic, see section 6.4.4.) If underspecification is used to handle alternative realizations, then the distinction between the three types of [f] will also appear in the lexical representations, as I will show in my preferred analysis of Gaelic lenition in Chapter 6. Similarly, lenited forms of /tʰ/ and /s/ realized as [x] may have the same realization as /kʰ/, as in *thulaichean* [xuɬuçin] 'of peaks', *shlios* [xliːs] 'flank' and *choireachan* [xɔrəxən̩] 'steep', the genitive plural of *coireachan* with radical initial [kʰ]. (For examples of spoken Skye Gaelic in poetry recitation, see Lodge, 2003b.)

Another example of the unnecessary identification of phonemes is furnished by English regular verb morphology (cf. Mohanan's view above). The contrasts involved are very few and are ideally suited to an underspecification treatment. The third person singular present tense ending is simply specified as [fricative]. (This is the lexical specification I give for both onset and coda /z/ in Lodge, 1992: 29, Fig. 1.) In terms of concatenation a vocoid articulation [ɪ] occurs automatically when the coda of the last syllable of the stem is also specified as [fricative], which is the specification of all the sibilants but not of the other fricatives in my analysis in Lodge (1992). There are also assimilated palato-alveolar realizations to be accounted for, but I do not intend to deal with them here (see, however, Lodge, 1992: 38–40). Otherwise the place feature is supplied by default as alveolar.

Phonation is determined by the preceding coda consonant. This can be determined by spreading. If one postulates a general spreading mechanism along the lines of (3.3), then we still need to know in any particular instance in which direction the spreading should proceed in those cases where there are two possibilities.

(3.3)   Spread lexically specified features into any adjacent empty syllable slots

In English, different articulatory parameters are affected in different ways: phonation spreading goes from left to right, place spreading from right to left. (That such spreading characteristics may be determined in either a language- or parameter-specific way needs investigation.) Note that the phenomenon referred to here as spreading is part of the phonetic implementation component of the grammar, which interprets the phonological structures of the language (see further, section 6.2). The default feature of velic position is [oral].

The past tense marker must be left totally unspecified. This is because it alternates with zero when flanked by other consonants, as in *changed me, pushed me*. (This is true of any [t] and [d] in non-verbal environments as well, as in *just right, lifts*; cf. Lodge, 1984: 9–10.) If the realization is not zero, then there are a number of options: spread of the stem-final features, assimilation to the following consonant, or a coronal stop, as in (3.4), respectively.

(3.4)   [puʃʃ mɪ], [puʃˀpˀ mɪ], [puʃˀtˀ mɪ]

Left-to-right spreading is language-specific; if there is a stop realization, however, the phonation is glottal closure rather than voicelessness. Again, default features [stop] and [alveolar] are supplied, if assimilation does not take place.

Finally, the present participle ending is simply specified as [nasal]. The obligatory vocoid [ɪ] does not have to be lexically specified. Many accents of English apply the default place as alveolarity, giving [ɪn], but standard English has a default specification of [dorsal] in this morphological context. A universal default statement, (3.5), supplies the phonation feature, in which the left-hand side of the statement indicates the relevant feature layer (see further, section 6.2 below; in Lodge, 1992: 26, I use a somewhat different formulation).

(3.5)   PHONATION → [voiced]

It seems to me that there is no reason to appeal to any kind of identification of these realizations with phonemes that are found in other parts of the phonological system of English. It is surely the spelling system in particular which encourages us to do so. The process of learning to read automatically involves learning to segment, but reading is not determined by an innate mechanism, otherwise we would not need to be taught it. Is it necessarily the case that children make the identification of onsets and codas that most linguists assume? What evidence have we that English children associate coda [ʔ] with onset [p t k], as appropriate, until they learn to spell? Or that Greek children analyze [b] in [ti borta] την πορτα 'the door' (accusative) as /-n p-/ or [g] in [ti gori] την κορη 'the daughter' (acc.) as /-n k-/, until they too learn to spell? (Cf. Newton's, 1970 and Ferguson's, 1978 comments on Modern Greek, as well as the work of Morais, 1991 and Morais et al., 1986, on the rôle of reading and writing in learning to segment, to which we return in Chapter 4.)

In Chapter 5 we will consider the matter of phonetic interpretation of phonological structures and instances of mixing up the two levels. This potential mixing up of phonetic and phonological terminology can be seen in Gussmann's presentation of Icelandic data, in particular in relation to aspirated stops (to which we return in Chapter 4), and relates to the issue of identifying realizations as 'the same'. We are told that 'aspirated plosives can only appear in the onset' (2002: 179); in fact, this is a crucial distinguishing characteristic of these sounds in Icelandic. But is this a statement about realizations or phonological structure? Gussmann demonstrates that aspirated plosives cannot combine with any other obstruents in sequence; he provides examples of alternations in adjectives (ibid.: 135) between masculine and neuter forms respectively, as in (3.6).

(3.6)   [riːkʰʏr]   [rixt]   rich
         [tjuːpʰʏr]   [tjuft]   deep

Since these are alternations in one and the same morpheme, then why not equate the alternating forms as realizations of the same phonological entity? Past tense forms work in the same way: the preterite suffix [tʰɪ] (ibid.: 136) produces alternate forms *vis-à-vis* the infinitive, as in (3.7), where the suffix consonant is not postaspirated.

(3.7)   [vaːkʰa]   [vaxtɪ]   be awake
         [lɛːpʰja]   [laftɪ]   lap up

But we are told that such an association of the two realizations, stop and fricative, is not phonological (say, via lenition) but lexical. Gussmann (2002: 137) gives two reasons for this conclusion. Firstly, because there are unpredictable vowel alternations in the verb forms, as in English *keep–kept*, the verb stems have to have different phonological representations. Further, however, 'since the shape of the infinitive has to be phonologically distinct from that of the past tense because of the vocalic unpredictability, there is no reason to assume that this different phonological shape should not include the consonants that are perceived as phonetically distinct'. This is a non-sequitur: in any case, the consonantal alternations *are* predictable and entirely regular in Gussmann's data.

The other reason is a misapplication of biuniqueness. We are told, 'If the rhymal spirants were to come from plosives through lenition, this would mean that all such rhymal spirants are really plosives and would amount to an effective ban on spirants in rhymal positions' (ibid.: 137). But this is unjustified; it is the alternations that are crucial in determining the phonological status of any particular sound, not its phonetic appearance (nor the spelling system!). The argument he presents against the possibility of having two different types of fricative, the alternating and the non-alternating kind, is equally unconvincing. Gussmann claims we will not be able to differentiate between those fricative-stop sequences that show no alternation, such as [cɪfta] 'marry', and those cases where historically the fricative comes from a stop, as in [scɪfta] 'change', where the spelling *skipta* still indicates the historical origin. But why would we want to include historical information in a description of the native speaker knowledge of Icelandic? The crucial issue is whether there are alternations or not; we are told that there are none in either *gifta* or *skipta*, so they can both have phonological representations with the sequence /-ft-/. On the other hand, [tjuft] in (3.6) and [lafti] in (3.7) contain the phonological sequence /-p^h+t^h-/, where + indicates a morpheme boundary. Furthermore, if we are told that lexically 'the stem in the past tense will end in a voiceless spirant and the plosive will be entirely absent from the representation' (ibid.), then we seem to be dealing with an assumption of full specification of lexical forms. All in all, the arguments about the representation of these alternating fricatives seem to be aimed at saving the statement that aspirated plosives can only appear in onsets. This is certainly true with regard to realizations, but phonologically it is at least questionable. In Lodge (2007) I argue for a differentiation of alternating and non-alternating fricatives in these instances, thus rejecting an assumption that phonetic identity has priority over functional relationships. The two phonological types will be differentiated in that the alternating stops and fricatives will have no lexical specification of the manner feature and the non-alternating ones will be specified as [fricative], irrespective of their historical origin.

If we take Silverman's (2006) position on functionally based classification of phonetic events, as discussed in the previous chapter, then the notion of biuniqueness based on some notion of phonetic identity is removed from phonological theory as a pretended measure of phonological identity.

3.3 MONOSYSTEMICITY

Closely related to the notion of biuniqueness is the notion of monosystemicity. Once a phonological contrast has been established at one place of the linguistic structure, it is assumed to apply at all places. If it does not occur in one particular place, this is just a quirk of the particular system. So, English has a set of stop contrasts /p t k b d g/, which we find in both onset and coda positions in the syllable. On the other hand, /h/ is restricted to onsets, /ŋ/ (if it is recognized as a separate phoneme rather than a realization of /ng/) is restricted to the coda. The examples of English plurals and tense forms discussed in the previous section are equally good examples of the issue of monosystemicity as of biuniqueness.

To start with, I will look at a number of instances from Goldsmith (1995) and other related analyses. He himself takes monosystemicity for granted in his introduction. In his discussion of five kinds of contrast (1995a: 9–13) he refers to cases of neutralization as examples of *modest asymmetry* of contrast:

> This involves pairs of sounds, *x* and *y*, which are uncontroversially distinct, contrastive segments in the underlying inventory, but for which in at least one context there seems to be a striking asymmetry in the distribution of segments, judging by the relative number of words with the one and words with the other, or by some other criterion. (11)

(It is not clear to me how 'modest' is squared with 'striking'.) This would presumably cover cases such as so-called final obstruent devoicing in standard German (and other languages). Obstruents are contrastively voiceless or voiced in syllable-initial and word-internal position, for example in *Tank/Dank, Leiter/leider*, but in syllable-final position only voiceless obstruents are allowed. In the lexicon there is a set of stems which have alternating forms depending on whether or not they have a syllabic suffix attached to them, for example, *Rad* [ʀaːt], genitive *Rades* [ʀaːdəs] ('wheel'), and another set with non-alternating voiceless obstruents, for example, *Rat* [ʀaːt], genitive *Rates* [ʀaːtəs] ('advice'). The very notion of neutralization trades on monosystemicity, if there is identification of the sound occurring exclusively in the one context with one or other of the contrasting phonemes, *x* or *y* in Goldsmith's exposition. On the other hand, Trubetzkoy (1936, 1939), the originator of the archiphoneme, did not make this identification; indeed, that was the point of the archiphoneme, it was neither *x* nor *y*. In the case of German it is a straightforward matter to identify the alternating forms with the voiced obstruents, for example, *Rad* is phonemicized as /raːd/, *Rat* as /raːt/, with a devoicing rule in syllable-final position. (Giegerich (1986: 80–8) takes this position, although he identifies the difference as one of [±tense] and uses underspecification in the lexical representation of the non-tense (voiced) set.) However, one still finds solutions that imply one phoneme turning into another, as in Fox's discussion (1990: 69–71), despite the fact that no contrast is involved. Fox states that the single phonological form (/rad/ in his transcription) is subject to a rule 'which converts the /d/ to /t/ in final position.' This rests entirely on a misguided recourse to biuniqueness and monosystemicity and necessitates positing an extra layer of morphophonemics between morphology and phonology. As a consequence, morphemes can have different phonemic shapes. But we have already seen the problems of this approach in relation to English *ten* in that phonemic alternations necessitate sets of morphophonemic rules, some of which turn out to be very cumbersome. The archiphoneme principle rests on underspecification and an implicit polysystemicity: /t/ is a voiceless alveolar stop, /d/ is a voiced alveolar stop, syllable-final /T/ is an alveolar stop, and all three are distinct from one another in their phonological definitions.

The same applies *mutatis mutandis* to the vowel system of English referred to by Goldsmith (1995: 11–12). What reason is there for identifying as the same the stressed vowels of *Canada* and *sanity*, or those of *Oberon* and *verbose*? The latter of each pair alternate according to Trisyllabic Shortening, the former do not. The only answer can be the automatic imposition of monosystemicity based on biuniqueness.

Steriade (1995), too, takes monosystemicity for granted. In her discussion of underspecification and markedness she presents evidence against Lexical Minimality, an assumption behind much work in phonology, which she defines as follows: 'Lexical Minimality: underlying representations must reduce to some minimum the phonological information used to distinguish lexical items' (Steriade 1995: 114). She shows that in Gaagudju and Gooniyandi apicals are predictably [+anterior] or are subject to anterior harmony, respectively, in initial position only, whereas there is a contrast between alveolar and retroflex elsewhere. The unspecified apicals are specified by default or spreading, as appropriate, whereas the contrasting apicals are fully specified for anteriority and so are not subject to these rules. This is an important argument against monosystemicity: a segment underspecified in position A does not have to be equally underspecified in position B and no identification between the two segments is necessary. But this is not necessarily an argument against Lexical Minimality, in the definition of which no reference is made to monosystemicity, because, presumably, it is assumed.

Again, she identifies suffixal /a, i, u/ with root /a, i, u/, which also contrast with root /e, o, ɨ/ in Bantu and Chumash (1995: 156–7). This can only be justified on the assumption of monosystemicity. And there is a similar case with Hungarian (ibid.: 164–5), where the roots *nal* 'at' and *töl* 'from' as stems in, for example, *nal-am* 'at me', *töl-em* 'from me', are identified with the suffixes which undergo harmony, as in *ház-nal* 'at the house', *ház-tol* 'from the house' versus *kép-nel* 'at the picture', *kép-töl* 'from the picture'. The latter can be unspecified for [back], the former lexically specified as [+back] and [–back], respectively. Allowing vowels to be underspecified in some cases and not others explains the difference between the two types of morpheme perfectly well, provided we give up our insistence on monosystemicity. In Lodge (1993: 487–90), for example, I specifically do not identify the vowel system in the final syllable of Malay disyllabic words with that in the first syllable; the former is subject to constraints on tongue height depending on whether the syllable has a coda or not, the latter is not so constrained.

Interestingly enough, Itô & Mester (1995) distinguish between four phonologically motivated types of vocabulary in Japanese, comparable to the distinction in English between learnèd and Germanic vocabulary, for instance. Itô & Mester's analysis is essentially polysystemic: the distribution of contrastive sounds is different in the various types of vocabulary. In their constraint-based approach, constraints such as the one on the sequence [si-] apply variably according to the type of vocabulary: native, Sino-Japanese, foreign or mimetic.

The most extreme form of polysystemicity is that explicitly argued for by the proponents of Firthian Prosodic Analysis (Studies in Linguistic Analysis (SILA), 1957; Palmer, 1970). The published analyses nearly always focused on particular grammatical categories, for example, the noun in Terena (Bendor-Samuel, 1960), or the function of a phonetic feature in the phonology of a set of circumscribed forms, for example, nasality in the verb forms of Sundanese (Robins, 1953), without any claim as to the validity of the analysis for the rest of the language. Thus, the simple examples of nominal plurality and verb endings in English discussed in the previous section can be given as instances of non-monosystemicity. A monosystemic analysis of English will (implicitly) claim that the plural marker employs the phonemes /s/, /z/ and /ɪ/ and tense and non-finite verbal markers employ /s/, /z/ and /ɪ/, the same as for plurality, and /t/, /d/ and /ŋ/ in various combinations. But the system of contrasts in the plural and verbal morphemes is small compared to, for instance, the onset contrasts in noun or verb stems, so functionally the two systems are different. For a polysystemic approach to such phenomena, see Kelly & Local (1989) and Ogden (1997, 1999).

A revival of the polysystemic approach can be seen in the work of Silverman (2006), but from a somewhat different starting point. He shares a functional view of language with the Firthian tradition but is concerned also with the way in which native speakers store and process the forms they hear. In his approach it is only alternating forms which constitute the basis of lexical entry forms, not complementary distribution *per se*, as most approaches to phonology claim (see Chapter 2 above). Thus, a dialect of English which alternates [t] and [ʔ] in words like *getting* and *get*, respectively, has a phonological system in which the two realizations are connected (they are 'allophones' of the same 'phoneme'), but a dialect that has no such alternations has a system in which [t] appears in onset position of stressed syllables and [ʔ] in other positions, that is, ambisyllabic and coda, and their complementary distribution is not significant. In other words the onset system is different from the other two systems (see also Lodge, 1992, 1993, 2003a and elsewhere in this book). In a monosystemic account this is handled by means of statements concerning the restricted distribution of phonemes, such as /h/ and /ŋ/ in English and German, usually without reference to grammatical categories.

English, then, has (at least) two types of accent with respect to the stop system, those which relate [t] and [ʔ], and those which do not. We will return to this issue in relation to polylectal grammars, a high-level assumption of monosystemicity, in Chapter 7.

Morphological subsystems may also be marked by having an

idiosyncratic system of phonological contrasts. The strong verbs in German exhibit alternations and contrasts not found in other verb classes. Umlaut and ablaut, for instance, have specific grammatical functions not found elsewhere; past tense is marked by a different stem vowel from the present, and the subjunctive II stem often has the umlaut partner of the past tense stem vowel, as in *kommen* 'to come' in (3.8).

(3.8)   present: *komm-*   past: *kam-*   subjunctive II: *käm-*

Different subclasses of strong verb can be established on the basis of the patterns of vocalic alternation. For instance, besides the pattern of *kommen*, which is somewhat exceptional because of the infinitive/present tense stem vowel, we have subclasses such as those below in (3.9), with the past participle added and an indication in brackets of the number of verbs following that pattern. (The number indicates the monomorphemic stems; prefixes are possible with some of the roots extending the lexical count, for example, *greifen, begreifen, vergreifen, zugreifen*.)

(3.9)   bleiben   blieb   bliebe   geblieben   (38)
         biegen   bog   böge   gebogen   (26)
         binden   band   bände   gebunden   (16)

These patterns are historically based and are the modern German relics of Indo-European vowel gradation (ablaut), found in Latin and Ancient Greek as well. Nevertheless the patterns can be generalized over the class of strong verbs and are distinctive of the class. Other class-specific phonological characteristics include the relationship between vowel length and the phonation type of the following consonant in the past, subjunctive II and the past participle. A long vowel precedes phonologically voiced consonants, including the obstruents, which alternate with voiceless realizations in syllable-final position, and a short vowel precedes a voiceless, that is, non-alternating consonant in the first subclass in (3.9), as in (3.10).

(3.10)   blieb(en)   [bliːp] [bliːbən]
         biss(en)   [bɪs] [bɪsn]

In other subclasses a nasal consonant follows a short vowel only, for example, *beginnen, finden, singen*. The question is: should the sounds that enter into such class-specific behaviour patterns be treated separately from those elsewhere in the grammar that do not? For a detailed analysis of the German strong verbs in the framework of

Firthian Prosodic Analysis, which claims they should not, see Lodge (1971).

As regards umlaut, the vowels that enter into the morphological alternations that exhibit it are in a regular phonetic relationship. That is, a back vowel always alternates with a front vowel, for example, [o]-umlaut is always [ø:], [ʊ]-umlaut is always [ʏ] and so on. On the other hand, it is lexically unpredictable, except in the case of the past tense–subjunctive II relationship of the strong verbs. However, there are also non-alternating front, rounded vowels, which cannot be said to be in an umlaut relationship as there is no back equivalent, for example, *fühlen, füllen, König, Käse*. There is no need to equate these with the alternating vowels in, for example, *Bücher, müsste, Söhne, wählen*, respectively. (See further section 4.2 below; for a suggested treatment using underspecification, see Boase-Beier & Lodge, 2003: 128–9.)

3.4 UNIQUE UNDERLIERS

It is generally assumed in phonology that lexical items are stored in a single ('underlying') form, as mentioned above at the end of section 3.1. This is a way of reflecting the fact that native speakers recognize which word is which and which realizations are related to which others. In other words, it is a representation of sameness at the lexical level. Docherty & Foulkes (2000) point out that this may not be an appropriate way of dealing with sociophonetic variation, and review a number of strands of research which demonstrate that many of the characteristics of connected (real!) speech that have been investigated by sociolinguists, acquisition psycholinguists and others are used by native speakers in addition to the purely lexical contrasts of their language; such features of performance are as important in acquisition and recognition as the phonological aspects of competence. The investigations discussed by Docherty & Foulkes have led to the proposal of multiple-trace models of lexical representation, in which the native speaker stores in memory traces of every heard example of a lexical item rather than relying on a single phonemic form. This issue relates to the approach taken by Silverman (2006) and feeds into the whole issue of lexical specification and panlectal grammars. I will take it up again in my discussion of panlectal grammars in Chapter 7.

The notion of a unique underlier is also connected with the so-called citation form of lexical items. The acceptance of the former does not necessarily involve acceptance of the latter, however. The matter of having just one lexical storage form for each morpheme is closely tied up with other decisions on phonetic interpretation, the level of abstractness in phonological forms and the establishment of criteria for deciding how to handle morphological relatedness. There seems to be a variety of forms of relatedness, which goes beyond the simple dichotomy of transparent versus opaque. The simple phonetically obvious relationships in English plurals and finite verb forms, and in German obstruent alternations are to be distinguished from German ablaut and umlaut and Celtic lenition (both of which may have historically justifiable phonetic explanations) and from relics such as *foot/feet* and regular, but limited, loan phonology such as *sane/sanity*. Some notion of generalizability may be appropriate in this regard, though polysystemicity does not require the same level of generalizations as monosystemicity. The proposals of lexical phonology try to differentiate between two types of relationship, morphologically determined relationships and 'simple' phonological rules. This is a way of incorporating a limited amount of morphophonemics into the grammar and keeps the difference between the opaque and transparent types. However, the types of functional relationship between phonetic forms, such as those given above, do not fit neatly into two categories. Some phonetically regular relationships are lexically unpredictable, such as German umlaut, and other relationships are irregular and lexically restricted, such as German ablaut and the remnants of historical umlaut in English. In addition to this continuum of relational types, there is the problem of what determines the morphological relatedness: is it the semantics? Whereas the semantic relatedness of *foot/feet, sane/sanity* or *took/taken* is clear, what are we to make of *ignore/ignorance*, where the semantics has 'come away from' the morphology in a way that it has not in a parallel pair *deliver/deliverance*. This issue relates to historical change and it goes beyond the scope of the present book. (For a discussion of similar cases in German, see Boase-Beier & Lodge, 2003: esp. 80–4.)

3.5 GENERALIZATIONS AND POLYSYSTEMICITY

The question has to be asked whether a polysystemic approach recognizes generalizations. There is a danger that if we claim that all subsystems in a language are independent of (but related to) one another, each instance of a lexical item will be treated as different on each occasion. Furthermore, we will have to guard against the case where the [s] in *see* is considered to be different from the [s] in *same*, *sieve*, and even *seap*, where the following vowel is 'the same as' the one in *see*. This clearly cannot be the case in native speakers' recognition of linguistic forms, but it does raise the question of phonetic sameness again.

In a Firthian analysis the generalizations would be made over a relevant 'piece', that is part of the speech continuum extracted for its grammatical significance. This might be the nominal forms of the language, the system of verb endings, or syllable onset position – that is, a phonological structure with general significance for the language. Identification of relevant phonological units via the abstraction of phonetic similarity applies to the setting up of prosodies (syntagmatic (long-domain) features) and phonematic units (contrasts at specific syllable places). The prosodies themselves may also be in paradigmatic contrast with one another over the same piece. However, the number of terms in a system of contrasts often varies at different places in structure. We saw above Steriade's identification of Bantu and Chumash suffixal /a, i, u/ with root /a, i, u/, despite the fact that the latter contrast with root /e, o, i/. Thus, the suffixes have a three-term vowel system whereas the roots have a six-term system. Both Trubetzkoy (1939) and Firth (1957) emphasized the difference in function between differently termed systems of contrast over simple phonetic similarity.

The guard against unbridled polysystemicity resides in the acknowledgement of phonetic similarity as a classifier when no other functional considerations are relevant. So, the example of the different instances of English onset [s] above would be handled under phonetic similarity in the consonantal contrasts: /f θ s ʃ v ð z ʒ/, as far as the fricatives are concerned. There are no onset alternations in English which would override simple phonetic similarity, so each instance can be classified by means of its minimal identifier [fricative] with no other lexically specified features. (For an underspecified analysis of English consonants, see Lodge, 1992.) I will return to the issue of abstracting phonetic similarity from the speech continuum in Chapter 5.

4

SEGMENTATION

◡

The phoneme is not a psychological reality. Rather, it is a cultural construct. (Silverman, *A critical introduction to phonology*)

4.1 INTRODUCTION: THE ORIGINS OF THE PHONOLOGICAL SEGMENT

I now want to turn to the matter of segmentation. This is not a matter of sameness and difference in the way that issues I have discussed so far have been, but it is an important background to phonetic description and phonological interpretation. There has been a long history of warnings against the seduction of the segment – for example, Paul [1890] (1970), Kruszewski [1883] (1995) and Baudouin de Courtenay [1927] (1972) – as pointed out succinctly by Silverman (2006). Later the concept was criticized by Firthian prosodists (see Palmer, 1970) and more recently reviewed by Bird & Klein (1990); the most recent exposé of the misguided acceptance of segmentation can be found in Silverman (2006). And yet it has for the most part been taken for granted in the tradition of Western linguistics. Even in the approaches that assume a geometry of the kind presented by Clements & Hume (1995) with autosegments that are claimed to capture syntagmatic relations in the speech chain, the notion of segments as cross-parametric slices is preserved (see also Goldsmith, 1990: 274–98). The notion of segmentation and its tenacity in phonological theories is importantly related to our system of writing with the Roman or other segmental alphabets (see Morais et al., 1979, Bertelson et al., 1985, Mann, 1986, Morais et al., 1986, Read et al., 1986 and Morais, 1991 on segmentation and literacy), and a survey of the findings of research into the relationship between segmentation skills and reading/writing is a suitable starting point for this chapter.

The focus of the research of Morais and others listed above is the relationship between a putative naturally developing ability to segment speech into phoneme-like units and the teaching and learning of reading and writing skills. Two important groups of people provide crucial information in this regard: illiterates and those who have non-alphabetic writing systems, such as that employed for Chinese. The question is: does the ability to segment develop over time without literacy, that is to say can it be 'an effect of cognitive development and experience with spoken language alone?' (Read et al., 1986: 34, referring to the research of Morais et al., 1979). On the basis of an investigation of Portuguese literate and illiterate adults, Morais et al. found that the latter did not have the concept of initial consonant or onset. The results of the experiments reported on in *Cognition* 24 (1986), all point to the fact that it is only after alphabetic writing is learned that notions of segmentation (this, I am assuming, includes the syllable-place notions of onset, nucleus and coda) may develop. So segmentation develops with training, and can be learned even by non-alphabetic readers (cf. Read et al., 1986: 43). On the basis of informal observations over thirty years of teaching phonetics and phonology, the present author would suggest that even literates do not all develop the segmentation skill to the same level, if at all. Many educated people have no sense of segments in speech, even if they clearly do have in writing; whereas, in answer to the question 'How many sounds are there in . . .?', *bed* may be easily seen to have three segments, the same question applied to the word *rhythm* produces a wide range of responses, some related to spelling, that is, 'six', some to syllable count, that is, 'two' (*rhy – thm*). Clearly, this is an area deserving careful investigation. We will return below to the issue of children learning to read.

Arguments in favour of the phonemic segment as the basis of all phonological structure are often taken for granted; see, however, the specific discussion of this issue in, for example, Docherty & Ladd (1992: 149–318 and section B). None of these contributions, in fact, refers to the work of Morais and his colleagues, but Cutler (1992: 295) points out that psycholinguistic research is unlikely to provide answers to phonological questions. Given that there are various approaches to language processing at the phonological level, phonology must look to itself to answer its own questions. Whereas stored representations must be abstract and discrete (Cutler, 1992: 290), sub-lexical units 'may be many and varied, and differ from language community to language community' (Cutler, 1992: 295). This would certainly give support to Silverman's view that the phoneme is a *cultural* construct (2006: 208). Although Cutler claims that this leaves phonology no further forward with regard to the status of the phoneme, it constitutes an interesting starting point for the debate.

At the heart of all linguistic theorizing are the notions of paradigmatic and syntagmatic relations in language. But there is nothing that tells us a priori that paradigmatic relations that establish the meaningful contrasts of a language have to be between segment-sized entities at the phonological level any more than at any other level. In syntax, for example, a 'segment' is usually word-length, and certainly morpheme-length, but it can also be phrase-length; the 'segment' is the smallest bit of the speech chain suitable for describing the patterns of a particular level. We segment speech in different ways for different purposes.

The general acceptance of segmentation of speech may well spring from two sources: the alphabetic spelling used by many orthographies already referred to, and the way in which linguists are trained in phonetics. It is probably true of all phonetics courses that students are introduced to individual sounds and their articulatory descriptions in the first instance. This, allied to the fact that some form of alphabetic transcription (IPA alphabet or the American equivalents) is used to transcribe sounds, immediately gives the impression that such sounds can be extracted from the speech continuum with ease. The fact that this is not the case either articulatorily or acoustically is usually learnt later, if at all. So, students learn to recognize, describe and transcribe the 'building blocks' of speech and then learn to string them together. The isolated utterance of a simple English monosyllabic word such as [ˌbedˌ] *bed* is made up of three 'things': [b] followed by [e] followed by [d]. For many purposes this will do, but it fails to take into account some fundamental asymmetries in the relationships between the individual phonetic parameters. The voicing at the beginning starts after the bilabial closure has been made (see voice onset time (iv) below in section 4.4); similarly, it ceases before the final release of the alveolar closure, as indicated by the circle following the [d] in the transcription above (voice offset time (ix) below). Also, the tongue is in position for the vocoid articulation as soon as the lips are closed for [b]. This is overlap, not sequence. Indeed, it has been suggested occasionally that consonants can be seen as being overlaid onto the vocoid articulations (for example, Griffen, 1985; Local, 1992). Anisomorphism of parameters is the norm, not sequential ordering. It would be a good starting point in redressing the balance between acknowledging anisomorphism and insisting on segmentation if the IPA did not concern itself with (an outmoded view of) phonology and discouraged the discussion of segments in phonetic descriptions (cf. the paper on approximants by Martinez-Celdrán, 2004, discussed in Chapter 5).

4.2 SYNTAGMATIC FEATURES AND SEGMENT IDENTIFICATION

In speech it is quite clear that phonetic features take up varying amounts of time. A well-studied example is nasality. Bendor-Samuel (1960; also in Palmer, 1970) deals with the problem of segmentation in Terena, where nasality has the grammatical function of signalling first person singular, as in (4.1).

(4.1) [emoʔu] 'his word' [ẽmõʔũ] 'my word'
       [ajo] 'his brother' [ãj̃õ] 'my brother'

The velum is lowered for the whole word in these examples when 1sg is expressed. Of course, it is always possible to accept that phonetically there are no segments, but postulate the segment as the building block of the phonology, an abstract system rather than a physical output. A segmental approach to Terena phonology would have to chop up the nasality into bits and add considerably to the phoneme inventory of the language (cf. Bendor-Samuel's alternative segmental analyses). On the other hand, this is not necessary, if nasality is extracted as a whole. This one instance of a single feature having a grammatical function, hardly a rarity, gives the lie to Clements & Hume's statement (1995: 268) that 'single segments commonly constitute entire morphological formatives in their own right, while *subparts of segments rarely do*' (my emphasis); this forms part of their argument in favour of the root node, though it seems at odds with an earlier claim that 'features and feature sets larger or smaller than the segment have a grammatical or morphological function' (Clements, 1992: 186). But is not plurality in English realized as alveolar friction, and past tense realized as alveolar occlusion (cf. Ogden's account, 1997, 1999)? As I argued in Chapter 3, it is only an assumption of monosystemicity that makes it seem otherwise; for instance, the [s] in [meɪs] is identified with the [s] in [hæts]. The question is: if we insist on segmental phonemes, with which segmental phonemes should we identify these features and on what basis?

German provides us with at least two problems of segment identification: /r/ and the umlaut vowels. I will discuss each in turn. All phonemic analyses of German establish /r/ in the inventory (cf. Kohler, 1977; Fox, 1990; Giegerich, 1985; Wiese, 1996). However, the phonetic realizations of many standard German speakers make the identification of this segment difficult in anything but onset position. Although there is variation between speakers, typical pronunciations are those given in (4.2).

(4.2) [baːt] *bat* 'offered'
       [bˠɑːtˠ] *Bart* 'beard'

Back resonance is indicated by the back vowel symbol and the velarization symbol in the lower example. Phonemicizations would be /baːt/ and /baːrt/, respectively. The feature of back resonance is (at least) rhymal in all such cases, syllabic in many, and yet it is equated with a post-nuclear coda segment. There is, no doubt, an element of history in such an analysis, reflected in the orthography (significantly) and, also, influence from those cases where a post-nuclear back vocoid articulation occurs with or without a following consonant, as in (4.3).

(4.3) [fuːʌ] *fuhr* 'travelled'
       [pfeːʌtˠ] *Pferd* 'horse'

In these cases [ʌ] can be interpreted as a segmental allophone of /r/. (German /r/ also involves the problem of abstractness versus phonetics, which I discuss in the next chapter in section 5.9.) It must also be pointed out that simply because there is something that can be identified as a segment in some cases, as in (4.3) above or in cases where uvular friction occurs after a short vowel, for example, [haχtˠ] *hart* 'hard', [hɛχtˠsˠ] *Herz* 'heart', it does not mean that the back resonance does not affect the rest of the rhyme, as I have indicated in the transcriptions, where the vocoid articulations are retracted in comparison with those without such resonance, for example [hat] *hat* 'has', [nɛts] *Netz* 'net'. In other words, just because we can identify [ʌ] and [χ] as segmented entities, why should we ignore the back resonance of the following contoid articulation and the retraction of the preceding vocoid? Once again, a segmental approach that did justice to the realizational facts would need a lot more statements of allophonic distribution with respect to both vowels and consonants. The fact remains that the contrast is rhymal in all cases. Whether we want to associate this contrast with the contrastive uvular trill in onset position is a matter of our preference for monosystemicity or polysystemicity, though there are many cases where such identification is justified by morphological alternations, for example, [fuːʌ] *fuhr*, singular and [fuːʀən] *fuhren*, plural, in which we have the same stem. But if we are to ignore realizational differences between rhymes with and without /r/, then we have to have clear criteria for justifying this. Appealing to some vague notion that such details 'fall out from the phonetics' is not good enough, if we are to take phonetic interpretation of phonological units seriously. (For a declarative analysis of rhymal /r/ in German and further phonetic detail, see Lodge, 2003a.)

In the case of the umlaut vowels there are two phenomena to distinguish: the alternations of back and front vowels in the same root morphemes, and contrasting back and front vowels that do not enter into such alternations. In the latter case we are not really dealing with umlaut at all, as we noted in the previous chapter: there are no pairs *für* 'for'/*fur*, *Käse* 'cheese'/*Kase*, and although *schön* 'beautiful' contrasts with *schon* 'already', they are not paired items. (This assumes that umlaut refers to a morphological relationship realized in a regular way phonetically.) In the former case it is not possible to claim that, for instance, [u:] and [y:], [o:] and [ø:], [a:] and [e:] all contrast with one another in forms like *Fuß – Füße, Sohn – Söhne, Bad – Bäder*, respectively, since the members of each pair occur in alternate forms of the same stem. I have already argued against excessive recourse to morphophonemics in the previous chapter, so it is not appropriate to set up a system of alternating back and front phonemes in such cases, which are then identified as the same as the contrasting phonemes in non-alternating forms. The phonetic realization of the relationship is simply frontness, not a segmental entity. To that extent, it is similar to nasality in Terena, and, indeed, is a feature of the syllable (cf. my comments in Lodge, 1971 and 1989, and the discussion of resonance in liquids by Kelly & Local, 1986, presented below). In this case underspecification of the lexical entry of the roots is required with the features of frontness and roundness attaching at the syllable level.

On the matter of identifying the location of retroflexion in a number of Australian languages, Evans (1995: 739–40) has some interesting observations, in particular that it is usually syllabic in nature and proposes an interesting 'autosegmental' analysis of the alternating forms from Mayali: [ɖaᴵʔ], [ɖaᴵaʔ], [ɖaʔ], 'piece of stringybark' without the encumbrance of multiple association lines, as in (4.4) (the right-hand representation of his (14)).

(4.4)

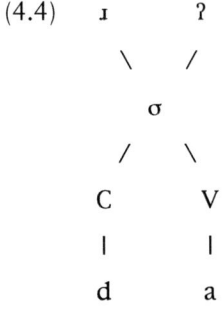

Insights of a Firthian nature may well have informed such an analysis (see Evans, 1995: 759–60 fn. 1); the distribution of the features of retroflexion and glottal closure is variable, but in each case they are represented by the same phonological structure. Further investigations along these lines is certainly called for. It does not look as though Evans's final prophetic comment on this matter has been correct: 'It is likely that the next decade will see many more subtle phonological effects reported' (ibid.: 740); few recent phonological discussions have questioned segmentation, though a growing number are revisiting the issue of the phonetics–phonology interface (for example, Docherty & Foulkes, 2000; Scobbie, 2005a; Silverman, 2006). But note, as my German example shows, we do not need to wait for further lesser-known languages to be described before we continue with this research programme.

The nature of long-domain phonetic features and their relevance to phonological analysis is well described by Kelly & Local (1986 and 1989). They demonstrate clearly that the clues speakers can use in identifying lexical /l/ and /r/ in a number of different English accents are spread over a considerable distance, namely from the stressed syllable immediately preceding the /l/ or /r/ up to the next stressed syllable. Thus, they mark the domains with underlining, as follows (examples from Kelly & Local, 1986: 305):

(4.5)   'Terry'll 'do it.
         'Terry'll be 'able to 'do it.
         'Terry'll be a'bout to'morrow.

Each accent they study has a contrast of front versus back resonance in the 'liquids' which is distributed phonetically as indicated by the underlining. The accents differ in the exponency of the contrast; Stockport, for example, has a front /r/ and a back /l/, Cullercoats a front /l/ and a back /r/. In the contrastive pair in (4.6) the whole of the underlined word is front ('clear') or back ('dark').

(4.6)   It's 'Terry.
         It's 'Telly.

Further investigation of such phenomena in a variety of languages is necessary. (Resonance and English liquids have been investigated further by West, 1997 and 1999, Carter, 2003 and Carter & Local, 2007.) Such findings have ramifications for the other problematic areas in phonology that I discuss in this book, in particular phonetic interpretation, abstractness and underspecification.

4.3 ACQUISITION AND SEGMENTATION

The issue of segmentation in the acquisition of phonology needs some discussion here. Only one page of Macken (1995: 688–9) is devoted to phonological units; we are told that 'from the earliest stages of word use, in most cases, children behave in accordance with the hypothesis of segmented underlying representations'. There is a nod towards Firthian prosodic analysis with a brief reference to Waterson (1987), but the point of Waterson's contribution to the study of phonological acquisition is missed, namely, that adults as well as children have non-segmental phonology. I have already raised the question of segmental identification by children in relation to the notion of monosystemicity in Chapter 3, and the process of learning to read discussed at the beginning of this chapter is particularly significant in segmentation training, but this does not relate to 'the earliest stages' referred to by Macken. On the contrary, as we have already pointed out, Read et al. (1986) conclude that the ability to segment does not develop with maturation but has to be taught. They investigated two groups of Chinese readers: those who had learnt only the Chinese characters and those who had learnt both the characters and the Chinese Romanized pinyin, which was introduced in 1958. However, it is important to note that (i) few Chinese adults need or use the pinyin alphabet (Read et al., 1986: 36), and (ii) even alphabetic writing is taught in terms of syllable and morphemes in China (Read et al., 1986: 42). The results show that even non-alphabetic readers who have learnt pinyin are poor at segmentation tasks, even though they can be trained to develop the skill. The results support those of Morais et al. (1986) whose work on Portuguese illiterates was discussed above; ex-illiterates, both poor and better readers, performed the segmentation tasks better. Given my own informal observations over many years, it would seem that further testing of literate adults is needed (as well as of illiterates); furthermore, it has to be asked whether tasks such as 'Delete the initial sound' (cf. Morais et al., 1986: 48, and Read et al., 1986: 36) are meaningful in the same way to all literate adults.

The assumption of segmentation in the earliest stages of acquisition (see Macken above) makes it a complicated matter to explain some phenomena which are explicable in terms of timing of the individual parameters of articulation. In Lodge (1983) I give an example from a 3¾-year-old boy, represented as [-ɫɫ-] for the adult target /lzs/ in *Mrs Neal's selling her house*. Rather than attempt the difficult

```
                           [-ɬ  z̥  s-]
          voicing          ------|
          laterality       |---|
          friction              |-------|
          alveolarity      |-----------|
```

Figure 4.1   *Adult articulation*

```
                           [-ɬ ɬ ɬ-]
          voicelessness    |-------|
          laterality       |-------|
          friction         |-------|
          alveolarity      |-------|
```

Figure 4.2   *Child's articulation*

timing and overlap of the features of laterality, friction and phonation involved in the adult realization as [-ɬz̥ s-], the child recognizes the phonological structure as three consonants but simply uses the three features laterality, friction and voicelessness all together for the duration of the contoid phase. Alveolarity is constant in both versions. I give parametric representations of this in Figures 4.1 and 4.2. If the child does recognize the sequence as representing three (adult) consonants, as I suggest above, then that is the level at which segmentation is relevant, rather than cross-parametrically.

4.4 TIMING AND SEGMENTHOOD

The duration of relevant features of speech varies and need not be determined a priori as essentially segmental. The skeletal tier of many geometries, equivalent to consonants and vowels in other classifications, is clearly a suitable segmental level of organization. We need to refer to onsets, nuclei and codas in making our statements about linguistic structure, but the way in which features are associated with this tier does not have to be on a one-at-a-time basis. The example of nasality in Terena and the resonance of both /r/ and umlaut in German show this clearly. So-called vowel harmony systems typically show similar non-segmental characteristics; see, for example, Waterson (1956; in Palmer, 1970) on Turkish, and Local & Lodge (1996, 2004) and Lodge, Local & Harlow (in prep.) on Kalenjin (Tugen dialect). It is interesting to note van der Hulst & van de Weijer's proposal (1995:

509) that in a syllable-head approach harmonic features associate with syllable nodes. This could be a clear representation of the syllabic nature of many such features (cf. Local & Lodge's Syllable Integrity Constraint, 1996 and their reformulation in terms of Declarative Phonology in Lodge, Local & Harlow, in prep.). However, van der Hulst & van de Weijer go on to say that such features percolate only to the heads of these nodes, namely the vocalic root nodes. This is a missed opportunity: far from trying to single out vowels as opposed to consonants as segments affected by harmony, they should assume that the percolation applies to all syllable places. This is certainly the case with many instances of features like lip-rounding and ATR. In Turkish the whole syllable is either rounded or unrounded: the operation of the harmony rules means that all three syllables have the same value in cases like [tytyndʒy] 'tobacconist' and [denizdʒi] 'sailor'. In Kalenjin, as I show in Table 5.1 below, the phonetic exponents of the ATR harmony system affect both consonants and vowels. Van der Hulst & van de Weijer propose a perfectly good representation of the prosodic nature of harmony and then continue to discuss the phenomenon as something that affects vowels (as per the title of their chapter). The only kind of harmony that would not necessarily affect consonants would be one based exclusively on tongue height (see van der Hulst & van de Weijer, 1995: 517–19).

As a general comment on the issue of segmentation I would say that the many gains of autosegmental phonology in terms of an appreciation of syntagmatic features seem to have been thrown away by an insistence on segments (see, for instance, Clements & Hume's concern with segmenthood, 1995: 257). This insistence on seeing things as segmental leads linguists to claim a higher status for some phenomena than is warranted. Take, for example, Clements & Hume's discussion of intrusive stop formation in English (1995: 272–3). Even though we are told that the possible oral stop phases in the codas of *dense* and *false* are shorter than those in *dents* and *faults*, with a supporting reference from Fourakis & Port (1986), the phenomenon of oral occlusive transitions is treated as the insertion of a segment. In Lodge (2007: 69–75) I discuss this particular phenomenon, usually referred to as epenthesis, an equivalent of insertion generally. The fact that this phenomenon is referred to by means of a noun, whether epenthesis or insertion, with a segment name attached to it, for instance, *t-insertion*, elevates it to the status of an entity that presupposes 'between X and Y' and that some other entity is inserted, namely a segment. In other words a segmental view of the process is implicit in its description. It is true that some, mainly historical, phenomena are properly described as epenthesis – for example, the medial voiced stops in English *bramble* and *thunder*, or the initial [e]-vowel in Spanish *Espana*, *espada* and French *Espagne*, *épée*. These and many other similar instances are examples of systematic phonological changes brought about by the insertion of what is usually termed a segment, with corresponding resyllabification of the form(s) involved, as appropriate. (See also Hall's, 2006, discussion of the relationship between vowel epenthesis and syllabicity.) Since the term *t-insertion* implies 'between X and Y', where X and Y are separate entities, the term further implies that the insertion is across all articulatory parameters. Once again we have evidence of the phonetics being set up to serve the phonology (for some discussion of this, see Local & Lodge, 2004 and Lodge, Local & Harlow, in prep.). Retiming of the co-occurring parametric features, which may also lead to phonological change, does not imply insertion of anything between two other discrete entities. In the case of nasal-fricative sequences the delayed onset of frication (slight opening of the articulators) gives a period of voiceless closure, but it is only the place/mode articulator that is involved. So the phonetics of such phenomena does not have to be translated into a segmental analysis.

The key issue here is the a priori assumption of segmental status for the epenthetic [t]. Hall (2006), in a paper dealing with vocalic interpolations within a framework of Articulatory Phonology, has similar misgivings about cases where the vocoid articulation is the result of retiming of the articulatory gestures rather than segment insertion. She, therefore, distinguishes between intrusion and epenthesis; in the case of vocoid articulations the former produces no extra syllable, whereas the latter does. So, in cases of insertion a phonological monosyllable such as Scots Gaelic (Argyll) /marv/ *mairbh* 'dead' is pronounced [marəv] with an intrusive schwa. Crucially this word behaves as a monosyllable; for example, it does not have an epenthetic glottal stop after the first vocoid, *[maʔrəv], which would be expected if the [a] was considered to be in a stressed open syllable, which has to be heavy, as in /u/ 'egg' = [uʔ], and it counts as monosyllabic in Gaelic metrics. The criterion for intrusion versus epenthesis is one of function, not one of duration, which, as Hall (2006) points out, can be highly variable and as great as for an epenthetic vowel. Indeed, in many Scots Gaelic words the 'intrusive' vocoid articulation is longer than the 'root' vowel realization, for instance, [gɔɹɔːm] *gorm* 'green', [steɹeːm] *stoirm* 'storm', [faɫaːv] *falbh* 'going'.

Compare the last example with one with a lexical unstressed schwa, as in ['fatəv] *falamh* 'empty'. The words with intrusive vocoids have idiosyncratic tonal patterns and are the only words that have the durational differences between first and second vocoid as indicated. They have a full set of vocoid qualities in the second vocoid phase, usually a 'copy' of the first one, though there is dialect variation in this regard. Unstressed, second lexical syllables have a limited set of vowel contrasts. (For a full discussion of such forms in Bara Gaelic, see Bosch & de Jong, 1997.) The consonants involved are always /l m n r/ (with various realizations, sometimes depending on the dialect). If the monosyllabicity is genuine as a functional criterion, then it is possible to interpret the sonorant as an 'interlude' overlaid onto the vocoid articulation, especially as the resonance features remain constant throughout the whole articulation (cf. Bosch & de Jong, 1997, and Hall, 2006).

Silverman (2006) also gives a number of examples of retiming of phonetic features in the development of phonological systems. For instance, in Trique, an Otomanguean language from southern Mexico, there are voiceless–voiced stop pairs with a three-way distinction of place. The velar stops have extended back resonance and lip-rounding when a preceding lip-rounded vocoid articulation occurs, for example, [nukwah] 'strong', [rugwi] 'peach'. This extended duration of these features is not found with other consonants, for example, [rune] 'large black beans', [uta] 'to gather'. (Comparison with other Otomanguean relatives shows that this development has not occurred in their phonological systems.) This has led to a situation where in Trique there are no sequences such as *[uka] or *[uga]. So any description of the language in terms of /w/-insertion would be inappropriate; [w] in these circumstances is not a segment, but an overlap, a retiming phenomenon. (For details, see Silverman, 2006: 135–43.)

As an example of extension in the other direction we can take glottal activity in Chong (Silverman, 2006: 79–80). In root-final position there is a contrast between 'plain' and 'glottalized' stops. In phonetic terms the former are realized as unreleased, for instance, [kəkɛːpˀ] 'to cut with scissors', [leːkˀ] 'chicken', the latter as creak on the final part of the preceding vowel phase, e.g. [kəsuṵtˀ] 'to come off', [kəno̰ːcˀ] 'nipple'. Here, too, we have feature overlap; in this case the glottal closure associated with ejectives cannot overlap the vocoid articulation, since it would totally obscure it, so glottal creak is used instead, maintaining the vocoid quality. This type of extension of a phonatory feature has relevance for another phenomenon: (pre-) aspiration.

Similar timing phenomena such as postaspiration (the delay of voice onset time until after the contoid obstruction is removed) and preaspiration (the early onset of voicelessness during vocoid articulations), or cases of so-called deletion, as in the lack of velic closure in a sequence such as /-nd+C/ in English are treated variably as segmental or subsegmental. The arguments for treating such phenomena segmentally or otherwise are not usually spelt out; for instance, it is simply 'usual' to treat postaspiration as a feature of the voiceless stop to which it relates, and to treat 'reduced' realizations of *hand-rail* as instances of deletion, that is, as [hænɹeɪɫ] in every case. But in many instances of this last sequence the duration of the articulation (three consonants) is maintained, but the velum simply is not raised, so the resultant realization is [-nnC]. It is, therefore, inappropriate to interpret lack of velic closure as segment deletion in all cases, and it is equally inappropriate to interpret early velic closure and cessation of vocal cord vibration in words like *dense* as segment insertion in all cases. To put the question in another form: why raise the timing of velic closure to a segmental level and not delayed voice onset? Why is [t] in *dense* more segment-like than the postaspiration in *ten*? All these matters relate to the realm of phonetic implementation of the phonological structure, and implementation is variable (see Local, 1992, for a discussion of timing variation in the context of speech synthesis; Local, Ogden & Temple, 2003 is a collection of contributions devoted to this whole issue of phonetic interpretation).

Gimson (1962: 146–8) furnishes a good example of how a phonetic description can be turned into a segmental interpretation without any justification, in relation to aspiration. We are told that /p t k/ in the onset of a stressed syllable are 'usually accompanied by aspiration, i.e. there is a voiceless interval consisting of strongly expelled breath between the release of the plosive and the onset of the following vowel' (1962: 146). As a description of the interrelationships of the various articulatory parameters involved, this is already a misrepresentation: to describe delayed onset time as an 'interval' that occurs 'between' a consonant and a vowel, as opposed to a voiceless onset of the vocoid articulation, sets the scene for the later segmentation whereby the aspiration is interpreted as part of the stop segment; for example, in initial position of a stressed syllable /p/ is 'voiceless fortis aspirated' (1962: 148), so not only does delayed voice onset time belong to the /p/ segment, but the phonation is aligned exclusively with bilabiality, full closure and orality (even though non-native learners of English are warned 'to pay particular attention to the aspiration', ibid.).

A similar situation obtains with Gimson's treatment of the so-called voicing contrast in English coda obstruents (1962: 90–1, 147). The duration of the preceding nuclear vocoid articulation goes together with differences in the duration of voicing and yet 'length' is attached to the vowel phonemes and 'voicing' to the coda consonants. It is only an insistence on segments that forces analysts to make such arbitrary decisions.

Before moving on to a consideration of a differential treatment of pre- and postaspiration in the next section it would be helpful to consider a definition of aspiration from a phonetic point of view. The phenomenon is often presented as a characteristic of voiceless stops (in particular) (see, for example, Gimson's, 1962 discussion presented above), and certainly when it is phonologically distinctive it is ana-lyzed in this way, as in Gussmann's (2002) treatment of Icelandic, which we will consider below. However, it is really one of the possible onsets of voicing in a syllable. The vocal cords can start to vibrate at any time after the start of the utterance. If we take bilabial closure and release followed by a vocoid, this gives (at least) the following possibilities:

(i)   [pḁ] = no vibration at all;
(ii) [pʰa] = vibration starts after the lips are opened;
(iii) [pa] = vibration starts as the lips are opened;
(iv) [ˌba] = vibration starts after the lips are closed, but before they are opened;
(v)   [ba] = vibration starts as the lips are closed. (Lodge, 2009: 56)

(ii) is what is referred to as aspiration. Clearly it is a matter of a timing relationship between no vibration of the vocal cords and vibration. (Gussenhoven & Jacobs, 2005: 4 define aspiration in terms of voice onset time.) With this definition there must be voicelessness followed by voice to identify aspiration, or vice versa in the case of preaspira-tion where a mirror-image of the options in (i) – (v) applies, given as (vi) to (x).

(vi)   [ḁp] = no vibration at all;
(vii) [aʰp] = vibration stops before the lips are closed;
(viii) [ap] = vibration stops as the lips are closed;
(ix)   [abˌ] = vibration stops after the lips are closed, but before they are opened;
(x)   [ab] = vibration stops as the lips are opened. (Lodge, 2009: 56)

(vii) is usually identified as preaspiration. This is a somewhat simplified presentation in respect of the phonetic details of individual languages, especially those claimed to have preaspiration, but the main focus is on whether any of these relationships of phonatory activity to the rest of the articulation should be interpreted as segmental in all cases.

(For a detailed discussion of the issues surrounding the phonetic interpretation of phonological features, see Silverman, 2006, Local & Lodge, 1996, 2004 and Chapter 5 below.)

4.5 A PARTICULAR CASE: ICELANDIC PREASPIRATION

Within a segmental approach, Gussmann (2002: 54–9) treats preaspiration in Icelandic as a segment [h], whereas (post)aspiration is a feature of the respective initial stop, as reflected in transcriptions such as [k^{h}viht] 'white' (neuter). There are phonological arguments why this could be so. In the case of *hvítt* there are alternations, for instance, with the feminine form *hvít* [k^{h}vi:t^h]; the final -*t* of the neuter form is a suffix. Another alternation is involved, too: long V + aspirated stop versus short V + preaspirated stop. (Note that we shall have cause to question the interpretation of the final aspirated stop in the feminine form in Chapter 5 below.) So, in a monosystemic phonemic account we could argue that /t^h/ had at least two allophones: [t^h] in syllable-initial position and [h] before another alveolar stop, which applies in morphologically simple forms like [fljɛhta] 'plait' as well. Note that it is only the segmental transcriptions that suggest greater duration for [h] than for [^{h}] and that we should be wary of treating such transcriptions as raw data for phonological analysis. The same applies to the representation of the predictable variation of vocoid duration, if it is transcribed as 'long' with a length mark versus 'short' with no mark. We need to consider the issue in more detail, including the difference between alternating and non-alternating cases of preaspiration.

There are the alternations, such as *hvítt* – *hvít*, discussed above. Such examples involve the coronals. The same applies to the other places of articulation, so that no sequence of two aspirated stops is allowed, whether there are alternations or not, although geminate unaspirated stops are possible. So we find [flɪp:ɪ] 'collar', [hat:ʏr] 'hair', [vak:a] 'cradle' (geminates in Icelandic are conventionally written with a length mark), but no aspirated geminate equivalents; instead we find both alternating and non-alternating preaspirated stops, as in [k^{h}ahpɪ] 'hero', [θahka] 'thank', both of which are non-alternating (cf. Ringen, 1999: 138, and Gussmann, 2002: 55).

Although we have a suggested durational difference between the two types of aspiration, [kʰviht] could equally well be transcribed [kʰvii̯t] or [kʰviʰt]. Here, then, duration is being used as a criterion of phonological status both in the case of aspiration and that of the vowels (see section 4.4 above and Lodge, 2007). Of course, it could be argued that in such preliminary presentations of data, an analyst may not want to claim phonological status for details such as vocoid duration at the outset, but it is significant that the geminate stops, which are lexical, are transcribed in the same way using length marks.

We first of all need to consider the regular relationships of vocoid duration throughout the phonological system to see to what extent it interacts with preaspiration. For the initial presentation of the data from Gussmann I shall follow his convention of using length marks and his way of indicating pre- and postaspiration. The distribution is as in (4.7).

(4.7)

long		short	
[puː]	estate	[lamp]	lamb
[tʰvɔː]	two	[hɣxsa]	think
[faiː]	I get	[stu̥lka]	girl
[luːða]	halibut	[kʰɣmr]	bleating
[faiːri]	opportunity	[pœlv]	cursing
[cʰœːtʰ]	meat	[emja]	wail
[çouːn]	couple	[mjou̯l̥k]	milk
[iːs]	ice	[θjoutn]	waiter
[θaːkʰ]	roof	[kʰljaust]	fight
[nɛːpʰja]	bad weather	[tʰjalt]	tent
[kœːtʰva]	discover	[pjœ̞r̥k]	birch
[flɪːsja]	peel	[pjahtla]	rag

The length mark after the diphthongs indicate a variety of possible durational differences. According to Helgason (pers. comm.) the transition in such long diphthongs is always early in the articulation and the second position is held longer than the starting point; what does not occur is a falling diphthong of the kind that is normal for English. What is important for our purposes is that [Vː] is longer in duration than [V], whether monophthongal or diphthongal.

In addition there are morphological alternations that involve vowel duration, as in (4.8).

(4.8)

[heiːm]	world (acc. sg.)	[heims]	(gen. sg.)
[hœiːs]	head	[hœiss]	(gen. sg.)
[saiːl]	blessed (fem.)	[sai̥lt]	(neuter)

[lju:v]   dear (fem.)   [ljuvri]   (dat. sg.)
[tai:ma]   I judge   [taimti]   I judged

The distribution, as represented in (4.7) and (4.8), is that vowels are long before a single (that is, non-branching) coda or in an open syllable, otherwise they are short. This means that vowels in Icelandic are monophthongal or diphthongal with various qualities, and their duration is determined by the environment in which they occur. This is certainly one solution offered by Scandinavian phonologists generally, for example, Vanvik (1979) in relation to predictable variation of vowel duration in Norwegian. This brings us back to the problems of phonetic detail and its phonological interpretation in terms of segments. Gussmann (2002: *passim*) talks of long and short vowels and represents them in syllable structure as two timing slots versus one, as in (4.9) (cf. Gussmann, 2002: 161 (9)).

(4.9)   N   N
           / \ |
          x   x   x

This implies some kind of phonological status, which does not seem warranted; this 'length' is entirely predictable, so is it not really a matter of realizational duration? (Note that in some of the southwestern dialects of Norway preaspiration like that in Icelandic is found; it is also the case that many Norwegians and Swedes have preaspiration as a realizational phenomenon, see, for example, Ringen & Helgason, 2004 on Swedish; for further details, see also Helgason, 2002.)

Duration before the aspirated stops appears to be different from that before the other consonants in that a preceding stressed vowel is long, even when another consonant follows, as in (4.10).

(4.10)   [fla:tʰa]   flat (acc. sg. fem.)   [fla:tʰrar]   (gen. sg.)
         [li:kʰ]   similar (fem.)   [li:kʰrɪ]   (dat. sg.)
         [ljou:tʰ]   ugly (fem.)   [ljou:tʰra]   (gen. pl.)

There are also examples where a difference occurs between the duration of the vowel phase before an aspirated stop and before any other type of consonant, as in (4.11).

(4.11)   [ta:pʰʏr]   sad (masc.)   [ta:pʰran]   (acc. sg.)
         [fa:ɣʏr]   fair (masc.)   [faɣran]   (acc. sg.)

In the case of the examples in (4.10) and the first one of (4.11) an aspirated stop followed by /r/ form a legitimate branching onset, whereas in *fagran* [faɣran] */ɣr/ is not legitimate. (Note that this argument depends on the assumption of a monosystem such that what happens in word-initial position is paralleled in word-internal position, too.)

If we accept ambisyllabicity and assume polysystemicity rather than monosystemicity, we can treat the distribution of vowel duration exemplified above as a matter of timing rather than as a matter of segmentation. If all intervocalic single consonants are ambisyllabic, then all the syllables preceding them are closed by a single consonant, resulting in the longer vowel duration, as demonstrated in (4.12).

(4.12)

$$
\begin{array}{c}
R \\
/ \ \backslash/ \\
N \quad C/O
\end{array}
$$

fl	aː	t^h	a	
θ	aː	k^h	a	
l	uː	ð	a	
f	aiː	r	i	
	ɔː	p^h	ɪn	open (adj.)
v	aː	n	ɤr	accustomed

Any monosyllables closed by a single consonant will similarly have a lengthened vowel phase, whether the consonant is an aspirated stop or not. If more than one consonant follows a vowel, then the vowel phase is usually short, which means the coda is branching and may or may not be ambisyllabic, as in (4.13) and (4.14).

(4.13)

$$
\begin{array}{c}
R \\
/ \ \backslash \\
N \quad C \\
\quad\ \ \wedge
\end{array}
$$

k^h	ɤ	m r	
p	œ	l v	
θj	ou	t n	
t^h	a	l t	
pj	œ	r̥ k	
v	ɪ	t t	width

In the case of ambisyllabicity, it is the second of the consonants that belongs to both syllables. This ensures that the first vowel phase is short, because an analysis of the consonantal sequence C_1C_2 whereby C_1 is ambisyllabic would predict a long vowel phase in the first syllable, as in (4.12) and (4.15).

(4.14)

```
                R
             /  \  /
            N    C O
                 /\/
     kʰ  ʏ   m r  a    bleat
     f   a   ɣ r  an
     h   ʏ   x s  a
     st  u   l̥ k  a
```

In the case of the aspirated stops plus a consonant, as exemplified in (4.10), it is the first consonant that is ambisyllabic and the second onset is branching, as in (4.15).

(4.15)

```
                R
             /  \  /
            N    C O
                 \/\
     fl  a:   tʰ r  ar
     l   i:   kʰ r  ɪ
     lj  ou:  tʰ r  a
     t   a:   pʰ r  an
```

It is now a matter of phonetic implementation as to the duration of the vocoid phase, since it is predictable.

We can now return to a consideration of preaspiration, which is given segmental and consonantal status in analyses like that of Gussmann (2002). Preaspirated stops alternate with aspirated ones; this is clear from examples like those in (4.16) and (4.17).

(4.16) [tɛhplar] 'dots' (nom.) [tɛ:pʰɪtl] 'dot' (sg.)
       [ɔhpna] 'to open' [ɔ:pʰɪn] 'open' (adj.)

(4.17) *fem.* *neuter*
       [tʰou:m] [tʰoum̥t] empty
       [kʏ:l] [kʏ̥t] yellow
       [kʰvi:tʰ] [kʰviht] white

How, then, are we to handle the apparent vowel shortening in cases such as [kʰviht]? According to Gussmann's account the voiceless sonorants in (4.17) must be in a coda (for him, a rhymal complement) because the preceding vowels are short, so [h] must also be a coda. He claims this is equally true of the examples in (4.18), where no alternations are involved (Gussmann, 2002: 56).

(4.18) [ɛhplɪ]   apple
       [pahtna]   to improve
       [hɛhkla]   crochet
       [fljɛhta] plait

However, since we have seen that stressed syllables ending in a single consonant generally have long vowel phases, the first syllable of the alternating forms in (4.16) and (4.17) and the non-alternating forms in (4.18) can be seen as being closed by one consonant, whether ambisyllabic or not, and the vocoid realization of the vowel phase is long. If we remove [h] from the transcriptions and use a voiceless vowel symbol instead the pattern of vocoid duration is evident, as in (4.19).

(4.19) [tɛ̥ɛplar]
       [ɔ̥ɔpna]
       [ɛ̥ɛplɪ]
       [pḁatna]
       [he̥ɛkla]
       [fljɛ̥ɛta]

Because the symbol [h] is used in all cases of preaspiration it suggests coda status for something which is in fact part of the nucleus. The only instances in which [h] is legitimately viewed as a coda consonant are those where it alternates with [tʰ], as in *hvít/hvítt*. Since the duration of the vowel phase is predictable, the phonological rhymal structure of Icelandic can be represented simply as (4.20) rather than (4.9).

(4.20) R   R
      | \\ |
      N Co   N
      | | |
      V C   V

The timing differences are then a matter of the phonetic interpretation of the phonological structure.

As in the case of stop epenthesis, the phonetic material may be misleading, if we have no criteria for deciding on the phonological status of the voiceless vocoid phases. Once again we might wish to know if there is a dividing line in milliseconds between postaspiration ([tʰaːla] 'to talk'), preaspiration ([fljɛhta]) and morphologically conditioned preaspiration ([kʰviht]). But in the long run, the phonological analysis will be guided by the functional relationships between the various realizations of morphemes, whether alternating or not.

In the case of Icelandic, what Gussmann chooses to represent as [h] should be interpreted as a voiceless offset of the vowel before a voiceless 'aspirated' stop in the non-alternating cases, and as a predictable variant of /tʰ/ before another /tʰ/. If we abandon monosystemicity, as argued for in Chapter 3 and by Local (1992), Lodge (1992, 1993, 2003a, 2007) and Silverman (2006), then it is only alternating forms that are in any kind of phonological relationship with one another; in other words, simple complementary distribution with no morphologically triggered alternations is not a basis of phonological identity, and therefore is not necessarily a criterion for segmental status. I will return to a treatment of these phenomena in Icelandic in Chapter 6.

4.6 IRISH RESONANCE

Gussmann also discusses Muskerry Irish (2002: 7–11) in order to cast 'some initial doubt on the view of speech which the notion of the segment entails' (8). Promising! But the point being made is that 'segments are only partially independent of each other in a string and a degree of mutual interaction – or interdependence – is to be expected' (ibid.). So, we are being prepared for dependences of various kinds, syllabification, licensing, feature sharing, phonotactic constraints, but not phonologically relevant prosodic features. The phenomenon under discussion is the distribution of palatalized and velarized laterals: surrounded by velarized consonants (unmarked in the transcriptions) [ɑ] occurs, whereas when flanked by palatalized consonants [a] occurs, as in (4.21).

(4.21)   [kɑpəl]   horse
         [bɑːs]   death
         [mʲagʲ]   magpie
         [əlʲaːnʲ]   island (genitive)

In other words, the whole syllable is either front or back, just as in the case of German umlaut or lip-rounding in Turkish, discussed above. This phenomenon also leads to morphological alternations; when the consonants in question do not agree in frontness or backness, then the choice of vowel is unpredictable, as in the forms in (4.22).

(4.22)   [kilʲaːn]   pup
         [kimʲaːd]   keep

In cases where related forms have matching consonants, as in some cases of genitive formation by means of palatalization of the final consonant, then the syllabic nature of frontness or backness holds good; compare the examples in (4.23), where some consonants match and others do not.

(4.23) [bɑːs]   [bɑːʃ] (gen.)
        [kilʲɑːn]   [kilʲɑːnʲ] (gen.)
        [ʃɑːn] Sean   [ʃɑːnʲ] (gen.)

([ʃ] has a palatal component anyway.) Further, there are instances where the laterals are in contrast and not determined by the vocalic environment, as in (4.24).

(4.24) [ɑːlʲ] wish [ɑːl] litter

So, at least in some cases in Muskerry Irish, frontness and backness are syllabic features. The fact that in other instances they are not does not alter this, unless we insist on biuniqueness and/or mono-systemicity. The resonance features of the syllables do not need to be segmented in order to capture the general statement.

4.7 CONCLUDING REMARKS

It is quite clear from examples of preaspiration, preglottalization (as in Chong), lip-rounding (as in Trique) and other features discussed above that articulatory features simply do not align neatly with one another, and that our letter-shape transcriptions beguile us into think-ing otherwise. The issue of phonological segmentation into chunks of speech of roughly the same duration has not really been resolved. It is still bubbling below the surface today, as can be seen from some of the references in this chapter. There seem to be two alternatives to dealing with our ever-increasing knowledge of the phonetic detail of spoken language: either we claim that it falls out naturally from articulation somehow and can therefore be left to its own devices, or we try to incorporate more of it in our phonological analyses. The decision to go one way or the other still does not determine whether we segment or not; nor does it determine where the dividing line between phonet-ics and phonology should be. How much of the phonetic detail can be encoded in phonological representations and how much should be left to a separate component of phonetic implementation? I shall address this issue in the next chapter. In order to do this as thoroughly as possible, I shall not assume that segmentation is a *sine qua non* of phonological analysis. For many centuries those involved in describ-ing speech have assumed that segmentation is a useful tool for analysis at both the phonetic and the phonological levels, as witnessed by the majority of published papers and books in the field, but I would claim that it is an unhelpful starting point for any adequate theory of spoken language. Much of the formal apparatus of mainstream phonological theories is required by the assumptions of segmentation, and some of it by the assumption of monosystemicity, the issue I considered in the previous chapter. Once we accept that speech does not have to be analyzed into isomorphic chunks, syntagmatic relationships in the speech continuum can be given greater prominence, as was the case in Firthian Prosodic Analysis, and once we accept that, say, the onset consonantal system is not necessarily the same as the coda one, we are freed from the requirement of using phonetic similarity on its own as a criterion of identification. 'Allophonic' variation, such as different durations in the Icelandic vowel realizations and pre- and postaspiration, is dealt with separately, but only once, in the phonetic implementation component. What is unnecessary is the interpolation of a surface segmental phonetic structure, as assumed by most current theories, between the phonological storage forms and actual speech.

5

PHONETIC IMPLEMENTATION AND ABSTRACTNESS

◎

> The phonetic interpretation of phonological categories is context depend-
> ent . . .   (Pierrehumbert, *Phonological and phonetic representation*)

5.1 INTRODUCTION

The issue of the abstractness of phonological representations seems to be consistently avoided in the literature generally. There is an assumption in many papers that phonetic implementation is not a problem and it is, therefore, not addressed. (This is instanced in the many contributions to Goldsmith, 1995, some of which I have already referred to in the previous chapters; this collection of papers has been chosen for particular scrutiny, firstly because I reviewed it some time ago, Lodge, 1997, and secondly it was intended to be a collection of up-to-date seminal papers on phonological theory.) On the other hand, there are specific references to the matter; for example, Harris & Lindsey (1995) and Spencer (1996: 141–4), though in both cases it is assumed that phonological elements *should* have a direct and seminal phonetic interpretation. In a footnote Clements & Hume point out that their place features '*labial, coronal* and *dorsal* have specific phonetic correlates just as other features do' (1995: 301). These are listed in the text (Clements & Hume 1995: 252 (7) and, revised to include vowels, 277 (41)), as follows:

Labial: involving the lips as an active articulator
Coronal: involving the tongue front as active articulator
Dorsal: involving the tongue body as active articulator

Phonological features therefore have phonetic content.

Elsewhere it has been pointed out (Lass, 1976; Local & Lodge, 1996, 2004; Lodge, Local & Harlow, in prep.) that there is a problem with such naïve phonetic interpretations of phonological features. Consider a simple example relating to coronality as described above:

the phonological status of the feature *alveolar*, its unary equivalent *coronal*, or its binary equivalent [+cor +ant], as a defining characteristic of English /t d n/. As is well-known, these three putative phonological units are subject in codas to (at least) place of articulation assimilation with a following obstruent or nasal (cf. Gimson, 1962, and more recent discussions in Local, 1992, and Lodge, 1984, 1992); in other words, their exponents in this respect vary in terms of articulatory place: bilabial, labiodental, dental, palato-alveolar, palatal and velar, as well as alveolar. The only thing these features have in common is that they are all indeed place specifications. Clearly, in such cases as this, phonological /alveolar/ cannot be equated with phonetic [alveolar]. Furthermore, if we insist on such a direct interpretation of this feature, then we need a complicated set of feature-changing rules as a consequence (cf. Chapter 6 on derivations).

5.2 ABSTRACTNESS, PHONETIC FORMS AND TRANSCRIPTIONS

The first thing to note is that I am dealing here with the notion of abstractness, that is the lack of phonetic content to phonological features and representations. It is not a matter of abstraction, which is a basic analytical operation in all linguistic descriptions; we abstract away from the data to present a system of phonological (or morphological/syntactic/semantic) knowledge. It is the way in which this system is represented and interpreted, and in the end how it relates to the sounds coming out of native speakers' mouths that involves the issue of abstractness.

Fudge (1967) is an early attempt within the framework of generative phonology to introduce phonological primes with no implicit phonetic content (with a reference to Firthian prosodic phonology, 1967: 11). He states: 'It is . . . dangerous and misleading to say that either articulatory or auditory features ARE the phonological elements, unless they correlate so closely that no facts of language are obscured by treating them as if they were the same' (Fudge, 1967: 4, original emphasis). The two reasons he gives to support his claim that facts are obscured if one assumes identity of phonetic and phonological features are the matter of biuniqueness, as discussed in Chapter 3, and morphophonemic patterns, some of which are 'counter-phonetic'. The first of these Fudge exemplifies with tone-sandhi in Mandarin, in which Tone 2 followed by Tone 3, and Tone 3 followed by Tone 3 are both realized as a high rising followed by a low rising pitch (1967: 4–7). The second is exemplified by the Hungarian vowel system, in which phonetic [ɒ] pairs with phonetic [aː] in a harmony system partly determined by lip-rounding or lack of it; they are phonemicized as /a/ and /aː/, respectively. As Chomsky points out (1964: 74; quoted by Fudge, 1967: 10), /a/ is 'functionally unrounded but phonetically rounded'. Fudge sees this as a convenient shorthand, but argues that 'it is surely the task of phonology to make classifications on its own terms, to state explicitly what these phonetic-sounding labels ("Rounded" and "Unrounded", "Long" and "Short", etc.) are a "shorthand" for' (1967: 10). The Hungarian system also contains a situation parallel to the Mandarin tone-sandhi: [i] and [iː] function phonologically as both front and back, another pair of features involved in the harmony relations. He then goes on to show how totally abstract labels – he uses A, B, 1, 2, a, b, (i), (ii) – can be used to define the phonological relations involved, and then interpreted in four ways, by means of four different sets of rules: articulatory, acoustic, auditory and recognitional. Leaving aside further details of Fudge's proposals, it is important to note in particular what Fudge considers one serious disadvantage of distinctive feature notation, namely that

> systematic phonemic elements and their systematic phonetic counterparts are treated in terms which are formally indistinguishable, and this often forces us to imply that one systematic phonemic element has been changed into another (Tone 3 HAS BECOME Tone 2 in our [Mandarin, KRL] example). This is not only undesirable, but also unnecessary, since we do not require complete biuniqueness in our phonology. (1967: 6, original emphasis)

The separation of phonetics from phonology is the key issue here. Again, quite generally, there is inconsistency in the discussion of the distinction of the two aspects of spoken language. At the lowest level this is reflected in the inconsistent representations of linguistic forms, so that it is often quite difficult to know what is being discussed, phonetic or phonological forms. The problem is exacerbated by the fact that in many cases the forms being discussed are (at least) second hand, from another analysis of the data. (For a lengthy discussion of this problem with regard to [ATR], see Local & Lodge, 1996 and Lodge, Local & Harlow, in prep.; this issue is also referred to above in Chapter 2.) In such cases it is more a matter of the philological interpretation of written texts than anything resembling a discussion of speech forms.

The whole matter of transcription has to be handled with extreme care. Archangeli & Pulleyblank (1994: 159–61) discuss the matter of transcriptions and descriptions of vowel systems. They warn against assigning symbols to represent the data and assuming that this process is preanalytic. They point out that there are generally two purposes that guide the choice of symbols in any particular instance. Firstly, a general indication of the position of a vowel in the system under discussion, so that a vowel represented as [i] is the highest front vowel in the system. Secondly, and equally importantly, a symbol will also reflect patterns of opposition and alternation in the language as a whole, so vowels that pattern as mid vowels will tend to be transcribed with an e-/o-symbol, such as /e/ in Akan, which has a lower F_1 value than the corresponding high vowel according to Lindau's (1978) measurements. 'In sum, a particular transcription constitutes a claim about a phonetic/phonological *analysis* of a sound' (Archangeli & Pulleyblank, 1994: 160, original emphasis). Interestingly, they seem to see no problem with consonantal transcriptions. But the problem is that in many cases analyses are carried out at second hand, as I pointed out above, so, inevitably, such analysis is carried out on symbolic representations.

Transcription is made even more difficult to deal with by the fact that there is a division between IPA-based and non-IPA transcriptions. (Unusually, Odden, 2005: 34–9, gives both systems, APA and IPA, and gives their equivalences; the American system also includes the (dubious) phonologically motivated features 'tense' and 'lax', a matter to which I shall return in section 5.6.) With regard to vowels there is also the difference between an assumed trapezoid or a triangular vowel space and the fact that all phonetic training has to 'cut through' native-speaker habits of identification. In English, for instance, it is important to remember that [a] is associated with the vowel in *pot* and *pod* in many American varieties, whereas in British varieties it is either the vowel of *man*, as in the North, for instance, or the distinction in the low vowels is between [æ] in *man* and [ɑ] in *last*; the vowel of *pot* and *pod* in Britain is usually [ɒ] or [ɑ] with neutral lips.

Since symbols are decided upon largely on phonological grounds, as pointed out by Archangeli & Pulleyblank, it is often the case that the phonetic details are of no interest to the analyst. This may be in order in some instances, but ignoring the phonetic details can lead to misleading analyses, as suggested by Fudge (1967). In so-called ATR harmony systems (see further section 5.4 below) the relationship between the vowel sets is crucial in determining the phonological structure, so which vowel pairs with which other vowel is a matter of morphological alternations (see also the discussion of tenseness in section 5.6 below). But then the relationship is also seen in phonetic terms, so a single phonetic feature is made to carry the relationship, for example, [±ATR], [±tense]. If this is not a true representation of the phonetics of the language, what status and interpretation do these features have? What are we to make of Halle & Vergnaud's symbols [a] versus [ʌ] in their discussion of Kalenjin (1981), which is translated into [a] versus [ạ] by Archangeli & Pulleyblank (1994: 273–4), respectively? In terms of the arguments relating to feature specification, spreading and opacity to the harmony the exact nature of these realizations may not be crucial, but in terms of the establishment of a universal, phonetically based phonological distinctive feature, then much more needs to be known about the articulations and acoustics involved, as Local & Lodge (1996, 2004) show.

5.3 A CONFUSION OF LEVELS

As a consequence of trying to establish universal, phonetically interpretable phonological features there may be a confusion of levels in some analyses of the kind referred to in the previous section. Gussmann's account of preaspiration in Icelandic, discussed in Chapter 4, is based on the assumption that codas are rhymal complements, and that many word-final consonants are onsets of empty nuclei (cf. GP generally, as in Harris, 1994). This is the case with the aspirated stops /pʰ tʰ kʰ/, which 'can only appear in the onset' (Gussmann, 2002: 179 and *passim*). Part of the evidence for this claim is the length of the vowel preceding such stops: the preceding vowel is always long, even in monosyllables. Consequently, [θa:kʰ] 'roof' and [θa:kʰa] 'genitive plural' have the same syllable structure: they are both disyllabic, the former with an empty nucleus. However, some of the data relating to the aspirated stops seem to contradict the generalization made by Gussmann about their restricted occurrence. This is because it is not clear whether the restriction is intended to be realizational or underlying, so some of the discussion in Gussmann's analysis deserves closer attention.

There are the morphological alternations such as those given in (4.16) and (4.17) above, reproduced here as (5.1) and (5.2) respectively.

(5.1) [tɛhplar] 'dots' (nom.) [tɛ:pʰɪtl] 'dot' (sg.)
       [ɔhpna] 'to open'   [ɔ:pʰɪn] 'open' (adj.)

(5.2)   *fem.*   *neuter*
    [tʰouːm]   [tʰoum̥t] empty
    [kɣːl]   [kɣl̥t] yellow
    [kʰviːtʰ]   [kʰviht] white

The preaspirated stop alternates with an aspirated one in the same morpheme, but the vowel length alternates, too, just as in the case of *hvít* discussed above. If we assume that the alternating relationship between the two stop realizations is part of the phonology, then this means that underlying aspirated stops do occur in coda position, realized as preaspirated ones. Otherwise, if the final stop of the forms in (5.2) was an onset, the vowel phases would be long, as in the unsuffixed forms. Gussmann's transcription of these stops is inconsistent. Transcriptions such as [kʰviːtʰ] above have an indication of final aspiration (whatever that is; see below), whereas [tʰoum̥t] does not, though we are told by Gussmann (2002: 55) that the suffix is [tʰ].

Given our discussion of aspiration in general phonetic terms in section 4.4 above, one has to ask what traditional transcriptions such as [θaːkʰ] and [kʰviːtʰ] with a final indication of postaspiration are intended to signify. Presumably, such transcriptions represent a voiceless release, which is not postaspiration in terms of the second of the possibilities outlined in the list in 4.4 (see p. 55), which involves subsequent vibration of the vocal cords. A definition of postaspiration in terms of voiceless release suits a monosystemic phonological analysis of series of onset and coda aspirated stops as the same phonologically depending on place of articulation. However, it is more difficult to see what Gussmann (2002: 179) is referring to with transcriptions such as [tʰaːpʰs] 'loss' (genitive). (Similar instances of superscript *h* before [s] are given in brackets by Gussmann, 2002: 138, presumably to indicate optionality.) Before a voiceless fricative it seems unlikely that speakers of Icelandic release a coda stop, even optionally (Helgason, pers. comm., who finds such an articulation at odds with his experience of Icelandic speakers). Presumably, the explanation for giving transcriptions that are so difficult to interpret is the required phonological analysis involving identification of these stops as the same unit ('phoneme'), so the symbol that is appropriate for onsets is used in other environments. Which means these are not necessarily phonetic transcriptions. In fact, we need to know what phonetic cues there are for knowing that a final released stop is either aspirated or unaspirated, since both are released. We are specifically told that in words like *hvítt* the final stop of the neuter morpheme is unaspirated but with preaspiration (Gussmann 2002: 55, 134), so one might ask how it is that the neuter ending is identified as [tʰ] (55) other than by spelling, as a reflection of history. Note that in the case of the neuter adjectives Gussmann does not use the symbol for aspiration, as in (5.2) above.

So, in the case of the neuter suffix ([tʰ]) we have identification based on monosystemicity and are told that 'a sequence of a sonorant followed by an aspirated stop is pronounced as a voiceless sonorant followed by an unaspirated plosive' (ibid.). In the last example 'a potential geminate consisting of aspirated plosives is realised as a preaspirated plosive without postaspiration' (ibid.), but note that in the instances in (5.2), unlike in [θaːkʰ] above, the same symbol is not used in each environment. The formulation of this generalization ('is pronounced/realised as') implies a separation of phonetics and phonology, but using the same terminology. So, something is at one and the same time aspirated and unaspirated. In traditional phonemic terminology, which Gussmann eschews, [tʰ-] and [-̥ t] are allophones of the same phoneme, an aspirated dental stop. So we are still left with the question of whether the statement relating to the positional restriction of aspirated stops is a statement about realizations or phonological structure. This potential mixing up of phonetic and phonological terminology can be seen in other instances of Gussmann's presentation, which we discussed in section 3.2 on morphophonemic alternations.

In Blevins' discussion of the syllable (1995: 206–44) some transcriptions have square brackets, others do not. What are we to make of representations like Beijing Chinese **ní-kè-xùn** (English *Nixon*) without square brackets (1995: 228)? Presumably **x** is not intended to represent a voiceless velar fricative, though ŋ in **ní-kè-sōŋ**, an alternative pronunciation, represents a velar nasal. And again, what are we to make of statements like '[fɔɹmŏmɪnʔt] can be realized as [fɔɹmmɪnʔt]' (1995: 233)? One phonetic form realized as another? Steriade (1995: 154 and 172 fn. 41) refers to the feature [retroflex] in Latin, but in the footnote the discussion slips into being about the feature [rhotic] without comment. Tautologous statements also ensue from this confusion of levels referred to by Fudge: Macken (1995: 688) informs us 'that the surface [d] is distinct from the affricate /dʒ/'. How could it not be? The former is represented as a phonetic entity, the latter as a phonological one. It is equally true to state that surface [d] is distinct from /d/. (For the problems of an abstract analysis of English [ŋ] as /ng/ from a historical point of view, see Chapter 7 below.)

Furthermore, the metaphors used in describing linguistic structure become mixed up with the discussion of physical reality, for which different metaphors – phonetic descriptions of an articulatory or an acoustic nature – are available. This can lead to claims that are misleading: Goldsmith claims (1995: 6) that autosegmental analysis removed the abstract underlying segments in cases of absolute neutralization. In the case of Hungarian vowels,

> if we posit a [+back] autosegment as part of a root that associates with affixes, though it fails to associate to one or more vowels in the stem, the autosegment is not abstract, since it *does* quite simply appear on the surface.

But surely this is sleight of hand? Even if we accept the phonetic content of autosegments, the abstractness now resides in the non-association with the root vowel(s), rather than with counter-phonetic underlying feature specifications.

All this confusing use of terminology, in particular, 'phonetic' and 'surface', makes one wonder whether there is any consensus as to the meaning of these terms. Rather than being a label for those aspects of speech that are physical, 'phonetic' has come to be associated with a level of linguistic organization (see, for instance, Kenstowicz, 1994: 59–64, which is pretty much a description of the position taken by Chomsky & Halle, 1968). Steriade assumes that surface features are the same as underlying ones and refers to 'phonetic representations' (1995: 117), and for Clements & Hume surface structure has the feature organization they propose for phonological representations (1995: 250). In Optimality Theory (OT) the output, according to Pulleyblank (1997: 61), is 'the sounds occurring in some fully formed utterance' and 'the output occurs in an actual speech event', but nevertheless both input and output are represented with the same set of features. Kager (1999), on the other hand, makes no such claims about outputs, though the implication is that outputs are part of the grammar, not objects existing in the real world.

Assuming that phonetics is a level of the linguistic structure may have been encouraged by Keating's (1988) paper on 'phonetic underspecification'. I assume that this indicates a non-physical interpretation of the word 'phonetic', but by using it Keating and others side-step the issue of phonetic implementation of the phonology. As a phonetician, I would want to ask what such a view assumes about the position of the tongue, lips and velum, for example, during the articulation of [ʔ], [h] and [ə], which, we are told, are 'permanently placeless' (Steriade, 1995: 135–6; also: 152–3). Such claims certainly suggest that at least some phonetic features have no relevance to phonology. At what level do we lose interest in the configurations of the articulators and/or their acoustic qualities? If there is a cut-off point, what criteria are there to help us with our decision? There is no indication of this in Goldsmith (1995) or most other work on phonological analysis, introductory or otherwise. However, interest in the functioning of the speech organs is used when needed: Steriade, for example, claims: 'The unmarked value of any feature corresponds to the normal neutral state of the relevant articulator' (1995: 119); unfortunately, she claims that the default position of the velum corresponds to [-nas], despite the fact that in normal breathing the velum hangs down to allow air to pass through the nasal cavities. This concern for phonetic representations of a kind similar to phonological ones leads to the establishment of at least one extra level of representation, namely the phonetic one, but in many cases it still leaves open the question as to how the articulators are intended to interpret them. (See also Pierrehumbert, 1990, on the relationship between phonetic and phonological representations.)

5.4 ATR HARMONY

The phonetic interpretation of the feature Advanced Tongue Root is a good example of a complex issue that deserves further investigation in the context of the separation of phonetics and phonology. In particular I will concentrate on two treatments of the phenomenon: Archangeli & Pulleyblank (1994) and van der Hulst & van de Weijer (1995).

In their book *Grounded phonology* Archangeli & Pulleyblank introduce their first chapter, 'A modular phonological theory', with a discussion of the binary feature [ATR] in Igbo (1994: 1–3). Their presentation is based on Ladefoged (1968). The tracings of tongue positions from frames of a cineradiology film (Ladefoged, 1968: 38; see Fig 5.1) are used to establish a single phonetic property of two related vowel sets. The crucial data are as in (5.3), where the morpheme structure is prefix–root–suffix; tones have been omitted.

(5.3)   [o-ri-ri] he ate   [ɔ-pe-re] he carved
        [o-mɛ-rɛ] he did   [ɔ-sa-ra] he washed
        [o-zo-ro] he did   [ɔ-dɔ-rɔ] he pulled
        [o-gbu-ru] he killed   [ɔ-zʊ-rʊ] he bought

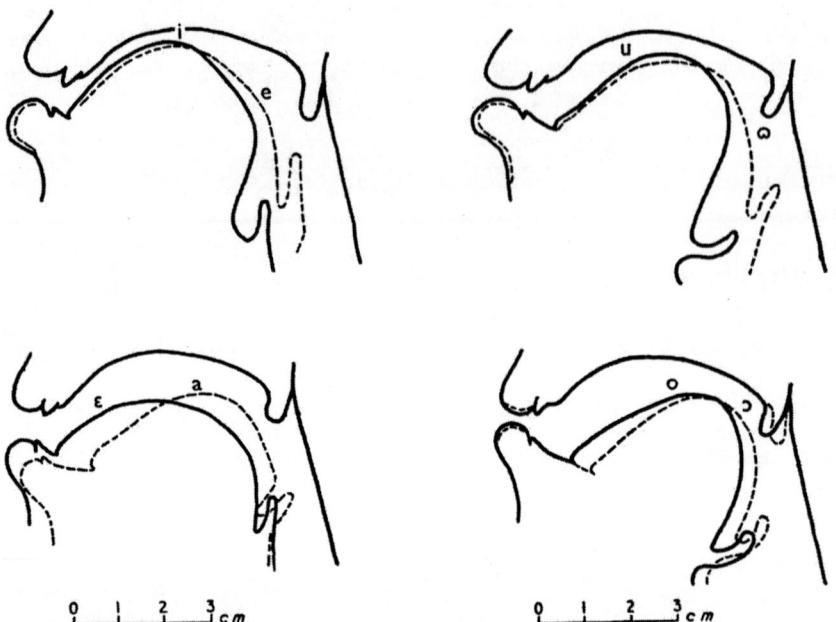

Figure 5.1   *Tracings from single frames in a cineradiology film showing the tongue position in the two sets of Igbo vowels. Adapted from Ladefoged (1968: 38). N.N.D. Okonkwo (Igbo, Onitsha): óbi, ùbé, ḿbὲ, ḿbà, ḿbɔ̀, ὲbó, ɔbὺ, íbu 'heart, poverty, tortoise, boast, effort, person, it is, weight'*

In the left-hand column the vowels are all [+ATR], in the right-hand column [−ATR]. The tongue body position is said to be 'relatively constant' for each pair. The two lower pairs show quite a difference in tongue body position, so maybe we should ask the question, 'relative' to what? We are not given tracings of, say, even English vocoid articulations for comparison. (See, however, the discussion Lindau et al., 1973, on tongue root position in a number of languages including English and German.) Tongue root position may well be an appropriate property to make the basis of the pairing system in the case of Igbo, though pharynx size might be a better way of presenting it (see below), but the particular associated tongue body positions in this case do not seem to be automatic consequences of the tongue root positions, so that any transfer of this property to other languages will involve language-specific interpretation of the phonetic correlates of [ATR], something that Archangeli & Pulleyblank later admit (1994: 161). However, they do claim that Igbo represents a canonical harmony system, which 'applies from vowel to vowel over a consonant' (1994: 8), so we only have to look at the vowels; see more on this below.

In Maasai (a Nilo-Saharan language like Kalenjin, which I discuss below) the pairs related by [ATR] are: [i/ɪ e/ɛ u/ʊ o/ɔ], plus and minus respectively, with a single low vowel [a], which Archangeli & Pulleyblank say is not [+ATR] and usually blocks harmony, as in the examples in (5.4) in which hyphens divide up the morphemes (1994: 150–2).

(5.4)   [ɪ-tɔn]   2nd person-sit
        [i-ton-ie] 2nd person-sit-applicative
        [ɪ-as-ie]   2nd person-do-applicative
        *[i-as-ie]

Clearly, the vowel pairs are different from those in Igbo, so a general statement of the phonetic correlates of [ATR] falls at the first example.

However, there are cases where the [a] vowel does induce [ATR] harmony, as in (5.5).

(5.5)   [a-i-ɲaŋ-ʊ]   infinitive-Class II-buy from-motion toward
        [a-i-ɲal-ɪta] first singular-Class II-annoy-continuous

In verbs with root vowels other than [a] the Class II prefix *i* is entirely regular in its [ATR] harmony patterning. This must mean that there are two kinds of [a]. Indeed, there is evidence that this is the case, since in suffixes the low vowel has an alternation of what Archangeli & Pulleyblank transcribe as [a/o], as in (5.6) (from their further, more detailed discussion of Maasai, 1994: 304–11).

(5.6)   [a-ta-dot-u-o] first person-past-pull-motion toward-past
        [a-ɪŋɔr-ʊ-a]   first person-look at-motion toward-past

(The past prefix *tV* only appears with Class I verbs.) Note that Archangeli & Pulleyblank's representation of the [+ATR] vowel of this pair (based on accounts by Tucker & Mpaayei, 1955; Levergood, 1984; Cole & Trigo, 1988) is the same as that of the [o/ɔ] pair. It is not clear if this identity is intended, though given the elements of phonological structure that they propose (F-elements in their terms) the two outputs would be represented in the same way. (In a footnote Archangeli & Pulleyblank, 1994: 461, fn. 23, they make vague reference to the phonetics of the [o]-realization, which 'could be derived phonetically or phonologically', though it is not clear what exactly they mean by this distinction, and one solution has to resort to feature-deletion.) It would be interesting to have more detailed phonetic investigations of the [o/a] pair, given what Local & Lodge say about the [ɑ/a] pair in Tugen and the overlap of [ɑ] and [ɔ] in the vowel area (see 2004: 9, Fig. 2), and the fact that from a historical point of view the harmony systems in the Nilo-Saharan group of languages have become phonetically and phonologically differentiated (cf. Hall et al., 1974). The Maasai system has some remnants of the low vowel [ATR] pairing still found in Tugen, but apparently with different phonetic realizations.

Archangeli & Pulleyblank (1994: 172–6) discuss the relationship between tongue body height and tongue root position further in order to establish implicational correlations based on phonetic compatibility, such as, if a vowel is [+high], then it is also [+ATR]. But there seem to be no compelling reasons why these two positions are not just dependent on one another and can be handled by a single phonetic feature of tongue body height or pharynx size. The discussion of the [+high]-[+ATR] relationship tends to focus on the front rather than the back vowels. Indeed, it is quite difficult to see exactly how tongue body advancement in the articulation of, say, [ʊ] in English or German can be accompanied by tongue root retraction, as supposed by its designation as [−ATR]. Given what has been said about symbols and what they represent, it is also difficult to know whether [ʊ] in, say, Igbo is the same as [ʊ] in English. (See also section 5.9 on the use of [ATR] in analyses of English and German.)

Because of their insistence on binary features Archangeli & Pulleyblank do not consider a neutral position of the tongue root. As with many articulatory mechanisms it is just as reasonable to view tongue root movement in relation to a position of rest. Lip position, for instance, is best treated as a cline, but if we need to label relative positions, then rounded – neutral – spread gives us sufficient phonetic information. In many accents of British English lip-rounding is largely absent, except in the case of [ɔ] in *thought, port*, though even this is not rounded in some northern accents; the phonetic implementation is between spread, for example, [ɪi], [æ], and neutral, for example, [ʊ], [ɒ]. Note that there is no IPA symbol for neutral lip position. Similarly, with tongue root position there is a neutral position of rest (cf. Lindau, Jacobson & Ladefoged, 1973; Lindau, 1978) from which the root is advanced or retracted. In discussions of [ATR] it is often difficult to tell whether [−ATR] is, in fact, retracted or just neutral. Van der Hulst & van de Weijer define [RTR] as 'retracted or neutral tongue root position' (1995: 511); a case of phonetic agnosticism or does the difference between 'retracted' and 'neutral' matter?

Van der Hulst & van de Weijer discuss the physiological correlates of [ATR] and tongue height (1995: 510), though their survey of
the literature on investigations into tongue root activity is far from
adequate (see Local & Lodge, 1996 for a fuller survey). Their desire
to equate phonological entities with phonetic exponents leads them
to concentrate their efforts, too, on features of vocoid articulation
only (though pharyngeal opening is applied to contoids such as the
Arabic emphatics by Lindau, 1978: 553). They, too, go on to establish some kind of 'ideal' or, perhaps, basic ATR-harmony system (van
der Hulst & van de Weijer, 1995: 511 (26); see below, reproduced
in (5.7)) from which actual systems are derived by (in some cases
counter-phonetic) mergers (1995: 512–14). They do not state which
language has such a system, only that a harmony system founded on
the [ATR]/[RTR] distinction '*might* have the vowel system in (26)'
(my emphasis).

(5.7) advanced tongue root   retracted tongue root
       front   back   front   back
       i   u   ɪ   ʊ
       e   o   ɛ   ɔ
                a   ɑ

In their discussion of the variant systems, many of which have only
one low vowel, they fail to make the point that the relationships
between the forms are the basis of an abstract phonological system
which is realized by different phonetic characteristics in different
languages and dialects. The system is not the same thing as the realizations; therefore, the mergers are of historical interest, but not surpris-
ing. Also, in the Nilo-Saharan group at least, it would be important to
investigate the consonantal exponents, too, given what Local & Lodge
(1996 and 2004) have demonstrated in the case of Tugen (see further
below, section 5.9). Incidentally, the kind of presentation in (5.7) per-
petuates mistakes of philological interpretation which are difficult to
eradicate: in the Tugen dialect of Kalenjin the [+ATR] low vowel is
[ɑ], the [−ATR] vowel is [a]; there is no doubt about this relationship
and its exponents in this dialect (see Local & Lodge, 1996, 2004). I
will return to a consideration of ATR in Tugen in section 5.9 below.

5.5 SONORITY AND LIQUIDS

One particular problem in this area is the status of sonority as an
organizer of syllable structure. If phonological structure is abstract,

how can sonority, presumably a physical quality of sounds, be involved at such a level? If, on the other hand, sonority is defined by reference to occurrence in particular syllable places, then we are in a vicious circle: sonority determines syllable structure and syllable structure determines sonority. The problem is made even worse by underspecification, since many of the features required to determine placement in the syllable are not available in underlying representations for the syllable algorithm to refer to. If features are supplied throughout a derivation (see Archangeli, 1984 & 1988) then syllabification must take place a bit at a time, whenever an appropriate feature appears in the structure. A particular example of the confusion of phonetic and phonological classifications in determining syllable structure is furnished by Clements & Hume (1995: 269), who assign the major class features to the root node of their geometry. These binary features are [sonorant], [approximant] and [vocoid]. (The last of these is described as 'the terminological converse of [consonantal]'; it seems more advisable to use *contoid* and *vocoid* for phonetic purposes and *consonant* and *vowel* for phonological analysis. I will return to this distinction in section 5.8 below.) Their rôle is to define the major sonority classes: obstruent, nasal, liquid and vocoid. Here we have a phonetic term, *vocoid*, a sound produced without any contact between the articulators, alongside 'liquid', which, for instance, Ladefoged (1982: 282) defines as 'a cover term for laterals and various forms of *r*-sounds'. This is presumably a phonological definition, as there is no phonetic content to the description '*r*-sounds' (see also Evans's comment on 'rhotics' in the context of Australian languages, where he questions its validity as a classifier, 1995: 729). Clements & Hume (1995) give the definition of liquid as [+sonorant], [+approximant], [−vocoid] with a sonority rank of 2 on a scale of 0 (low) to 3 (high). Even in British English /r/ has the following realizations: [ɹ ʋ ɻ ɾ ʀ ʁ ʈ r] (cf. Lodge, 1984), and in standard German we have [ʀ ʁ χ ʌ]. These two sets do not constitute an obvious phonetic class, and it is by no means clear how sonority applies to the *r*-sounds; fricatives are hardly in the same sonority group as trills, taps, approximants or vocoids, if the notion of sonority has a phonetic basis. (See Selkirk, 1984 for an earlier discussion of the sonority hierarchy; and Lodge, 1987 for a discussion of problems with the term 'liquid'.) German /r/ is analyzed as a liquid (Kohler, 1977: 157; Fox, 1990: 55) along with /l/; with the latter and the nasals it constitutes the class of sonorants. Fox (1990: 59) has it as [−anterior] as well. We can see the problems associated with a definition of German /r/ in terms of phonetically

based features; its realization as a trill or a fricative is hardly consistent with its [+sonorant] specification. And it is of no help to claim
that 'liquid' is an abstract classification (Kohler, 1977: 157) and then
use only those phonetically based features to specify it that do not get
in the way, for example, [-lateral] (Kohler, 1977) or [-anterior] (Fox,
1990) to distinguish it from /l/, because we still do not know how to
implement these feature arrays phonetically.

Of course, it could at this point be argued that establishing /r/ as
the phoneme is an abstraction from the phonetic substance and that
this is what is being argued for in this chapter. This is true, but unless
we have a clear statement of phonetic implementation, it is nothing
more than lip-service to abstractness. The focus of our analysis should
be on the contrastive patterning in the speech chain, in the case of
German back resonance versus its absence in the rhyme, as discussed
in Chapter 4 and Lodge (2003a).

So how are we to interpret 'liquid' in phonetic terms? Clements
& Hume's definition is hardly adequate. But without guidance on
interpretation such a term may come to be viewed as a *phonetic* classification, leading to statements of the following kind in Kaisse &
Shaw (1985: 6): 'Flapping, creates a non-lateral alveolar liquid'. This
refers to the flapping of /t/ and /d/ in American English, which are
hardly candidates for liquid status, as this term is usually interpreted.
We can see a similar kind of reinterpretation in the case of [ATR], as
discussed above. But whatever others have to say on the matter of
liquids, the definition given by Clements & Hume simply does not
cover all the realizations of /r/ in English or German, for example;
mixing up phonetic and abstract terms is not the answer.

5.6 TENSENESS IN VOWELS

A good demonstration of how phonetics is made to fit the desired
phonological results is furnished by Lass's (1976: 39–50) discussion
and rejection of the feature [tense]. (To my knowledge, and Lass's,
pers. comm., his arguments have never been answered, refuted or
even discussed until recently; Durand, 2005, provides further arguments for rejecting the feature, supporting Lass's position.) The main
points of his argument are well worth repeating here. His discussion is
presented in the context of English phonology and history, in particular with regard to the Great Vowel Shift, but is aimed at the feature
in general. Lass quotes Schane's (1973: 13) 'definition' of tense and
lax in vowels: 'Tense vowels are produced with greater muscular

tension, they are maintained longer, and the articulatory organs deviate more from the rest position . . . From a perceptual point of view, tense vowels are more distinct.' This description seems to be derived from Jakobson, Fant & Halle (1951) and Jakobson & Halle (1964), which Lass discusses later (1976: 43–4). Note that the 'definition' of tenseness is relative and comparative to laxness; no independent characteristic is given. Of course, many phonetic features are paired in this way, especially if they operate pair-wise in phonological systems: voiced/voiceless and nasal/oral are perhaps the commonest, but each member of the pair has its own positive characteristic(s). [Voiced] has a characteristic of vibrating vocal cords; [voiceless] has open vocal cords (cf. Ladefoged, 1971); [nasal] has a lowered velum, [oral] a raised one. Using a binary system to represent such features tends to lead to a positive versus negative view (and definition) of them, which, as I pointed out in Chapter 2, can be misleading. The feature [–voice] should not simply be thought of as meaning 'without vibrating vocal cords', since the system of phonation from a phonetic point of view has a number of different vocal cord positions, such as completely closed, as in glottal reinforcement, all of which are incompatible with one another (cf. Ladefoged, 1971: 15–16). Unfortunately, in the case of Schane's discussion of [tense] there is not even a positive, independent defining characteristic: tense vowels are simply 'longer', have 'greater' muscular tension and 'deviate more' from the position of rest. The physiological characteristic that gives the feature its name, muscular tension, has nothing to do with any particular subset of vocoid articulations. It is generally a component of what Honikman (1964) termed 'the articulatory setting' of a language, dialect or individual speaker. For example, in England speakers from the south east, including London, have a tenser articulatory basis than those from the north west Midlands, including Manchester (see, for example, comments in Lodge, 1984). This has certain consequences for the articulation of all the vowels (and consonants, for that matter); London vowels are 'tenser' than Mancunian ones.

As Lass is at pains to point out, it is the pairing of the vowels in English morphology that is the basis of this attempt to introduce a suitable phonetic feature, which in the end turns out to be 'The Emperor's New Feature' (1976: 41). The proponents of [tense] want to recognize the paired relationships of English vowels, which have been altered drastically from a historical point of view, but insist on being able to claim that the pairing has a 'natural', phonetic basis. Lass (1976: 44–9) looks at the matter of pairing vowels in phonological systems and the attraction of the symmetry that is involved. He gives the following ways in which vowels in a system may be paired:

1. a system of corresponding pairs in which each pair of vowels implements the same opposition (usually length), exemplified by Mangalore Kannada;
2. two sets of vowels in opposition as wholes with no corresponding pairs, exemplified by a 'long' set and a 'short' set not related by a single phonetic feature, as in English or German;
3. a heteromorphic system, partly of type 1 and partly of type 2;
4. a non-dichotomous system, exemplified by French.

Lass points out that pairing should not be an a priori assumption regarding vowel systems, but must be argued for. Treatments of English such as SPE take a system of type 2 (as argued for by Lass) and make it a pair-based system (type 1), and the crucial feature 'invented' for this purpose is [tense]. Of course, since features are universal, this feature then has to be applied to all phonological systems, whether they like it or not, as in Schane's treatment of French (1968) with 'pairs' such as tense [o] versus lax [ɔ].

5.7 VOWEL PAIRING IN NORFOLK

So, any pairing of vowels in a phonological system has to be argued for. Type 1 systems will usually be based on a single feature, normally length, so that each short vowel has a long congener of the same quality, for example, [iː] – [i], [yː] – [y], [ɔː] – [ɔ] (note, not [iː] – [ɪ], [yː] – [ʏ], etc., as is usually argued for). Type 2 systems will usually be established on the basis of morphological alternations of the kind proposed for English. Nevertheless, there is still the issue of whether the two sets are in fact allophonic variants of a single vowel set or morphophonemic alternations. However, I would like to show that it is not always appropriate to assume that it is the same set of alternations that is basic to a system in all varieties of a language (see also Chapter 7 on panlectal grammars). If we take the variety of English spoken in Norfolk, then vowels are paired in quite a different way. (This discussion is based on Trudgill, 1974 and Lodge, 2001.) The data to be considered are those in (5.8).

(5.8)	try	[tɟɑɪ]	trying	[tɟɑːn]
	see	[sɪi]	seeing	[sɛːn]
	say	[sæɪ]	saying	[sæːn]

do	[dʉː]	do it	[dɜːʔ]
go	[gʊu]	going	[gɔːn]
allow	[əlɑʉ]	allowing	[əlɑːn]
employ	[ɛmplɔɪ]	employing	[ɛmplɔːn]
know	[nɐʊ]	knowing	[nɒːn]

Note that the right-hand forms are all monophthongal; for this reason
the phenomenon is often referred to as 'smoothing'. (Similar forms
of 'smoothing' can be found in some types of RP, cf. Wells, 1982:
238–42.) As Trudgill (1974) points out, this phenomenon seems to
be triggered by the earlier occurrence of [ə] immediately after the
stressed vowel, whether a reflex of earlier /r/ or of the unstressed
suffixal vowel. In the cases in (5.8) we are dealing with the ending
of the present participle, in other circumstances pronounced [-ən],
and unstressed *it* [əʔ]. (What is usually written *it* could actually be
the unstressed form of *that*, which is used as the subject form instead
of standard *it*, for example, *That's raining*; see further Chapter 7.)
Examples involving historical /r/ are given in (5.9).

(5.9)	fire	[fɑː]
	fear	[fɛː]
	fair	[fɛː]
	tour	[tɔː]
	pure	[pɜː]
	store	[stɔː]
	tower	[tɑː]
	soya	[sɔː]

The last of these is, of course, a late borrowing with no historical
/r/, but would behave as though it had one, like *store*. Despite the
common trigger of this monophthongization, namely [ə], the two
sets need to be treated as having separate, but similar, lexical representations, because, on the one hand, the forms in (5.9) alternate
with a linking *r*, as in *fire/firing* [fɑːɹən], and, on the other, those in
(5.8) alternate between a diphthong and a long monophthong, as in
try/trying, in which linking *r* is not possible, *[tɹɑːɹən]. We have two
sets: the linking vowels in (5.9) and the non-linking ones in (5.8).
Even though there is phonetic overlap between the two sets, there is
no linguistic point in identifying such phonetically similar realizations
as phonologically the same if they are from different functional sets.
Furthermore, the examples in (5.8) need to be treated 'allophoni-
cally', as variants of the same lexical forms. Since such a treatment is

rather complex, I will not pursue an analysis of the Norfolk vowels in this book. However, one point needs to be made with regard to the regularity of these alternations. They are not restricted to a lexical subset, as in the case of the Latinate alternations in standard English discussed in SPE and Lass (1976); any schwa following one of the left-hand vowels in (5.8) will trigger smoothing, for example, as in *blue and (white)* [blɜːn], *to them* [tɜːm]. And one final point can be made here in relation to the Norfolk data: they furnish a good example of the anisomorphism between phonological vowel length and vocoid duration. In Norfolk some of the so-called short vowels (which are actually those that only occur in a closed syllable), especially the low vowels, are realized with the same duration as the so-called long vowels, as in (5.10) from Lodge (1984: 119–20).

(5.10)　[æːʔpɪ]　　happy　　[nɑːɹɪdʒ]　Norwich
　　　　[æːŋɪn]　　hanging　[ʃɑːʔp]　　shop
　　　　[kʰæːbnəʔ]　cabinet　[wɒːnʔ]　　want

Similarly, a VVV sequence, as in *trying, do it*, may have extra duration or the duration of a long vowel, for example, [tɹɑː(ː)n].

5.8 Consonant, vowel, contoid and vocoid

I now want to return to the differentiation of the phonetic terms *contoid* and *vocoid* from the phonological terms *consonant* and *vowel*. Whilst it is true that in many circumstances these terms overlap, they are clearly not in a one-to-one relationship. (See, for instance, Pike, 1947, and Gimson's discussion, 1962: 27–9.) Two fairly simple examples should suffice by way of a demonstration of their difference. In English (and other languages) what is phonologically established as /h/ is in fact a series of voiceless vocoids in complementary distribution whose qualities are determined by the following voiced vocoid articulation, as indicated in (5.11).

(5.11)　[ɪ̥ɪd] hid　[e̥ed] head　[ɑ̥ɑd] hard　[ɜ̥ɜd] herd　[ḁaɪd] hide

The phonological entity that these voiceless vocoids expone is, however, a consonant. This is established on non-phonetic, distributional grounds. In English consonants follow the indefinite article *a* [ə] and the definite article [ðə], whilst vowels follow *an* [ən] and [ðɪ]; the forms in (5.12) are not possible in any variety of English that I am aware of.

(5.12)　*[ən e̥ed]　*[ðɪ ɜ̥ɜd]

On the other hand, in Japanese voiceless high vocoids are vowels when they occur between voiceless obstruents, or word-finally after a voiceless consonant, as in (5.13).

(5.13) [ʃi̥karɯ]   scold
       [ki̥ta]   north
       [kɯ̥sai]   smelly
       [kaki̥]   oyster
       [katsɯ̥]   win

(See, for example, Tsujimura, 1996: 24–9.)

In French the same vocoid articulations may be vowels or consonants, depending again on non-phonetic distributional criteria. Consider the examples in (5.14).

(5.14) [uazo]   oiseau ('bird')
       [uat]   ouate ('cotton wool (ball)')
       [uiski]   whisk(e)y
       [uɔ̃ba]   wombat
       [iø]   yeux ('eyes')
       [iɔl]   yole ('yawl')
       [iœz]   yeuse ('holm-oak')
       [iauʀ]   yaourt ('yoghurt')

It is liaison that determines vowels and consonants in French: [z] at the end of *les* ('the', plural) before a vowel, nothing before a consonant. On this basis we can see which of the above vocoids are vowels and which consonants, as indicated in (5.15) where I have differentiated the two types as [u/i] and [w/j], respectively.

(5.15) [lez uazo]
       [le wat]
       [le wiski]
       [le wɔ̃ba]
       [lez iø]
       [le jɔl]
       [lez iœz]
       [le jauʀ]

(The liaison form of *les yeuses* is prescribed as obligatory, but since the word is highly specialized, many French speakers are uncertain about liaison in this case, as they typically do not know the word, so would have to rely on the arbitrary prescriptions of a dictionary.)

We can now, in (5.16), give definitions of the four terms under consideration.

(5.16)   contoid: having an obstruction in the oral airstream, either complete or partial, producing at least local audible friction;

vocoid: having no obstruction in the oral airstream, but employing an approximation of the articulators which does not produce local audible friction;

consonant: one of a class of sounds occurring in the onset or coda of a syllable;

vowel: one of a class of sounds occurring in the nucleus of a syllable.

Note that under these definitions approximants belong to the class of vocoids. Approximants and their definition are discussed in Martinez-Celdrán (2004), who is at pains to elaborate and improve on the IPA definition. It is a good example of an unnecessary confusion of purely phonetic and purely phonological matters. He points out that there are different subcategories of approximant: laterals, non-laterals (centrals) and semi-vowels (ibid.: 202). In addition he says that the 'so-called rhotics' could be separated from the other centrals. He also refers to the overlap of the 'semi-vowels' and the high vowels, as evidenced in [j : i], [w : u], [ɥ : y], [ɰ : ɯ]. The former in each pair is shorter than the latter. He discusses the phonetic differences between Spanish [j̝ j i], none of which have any friction, unlike [ʝ] (ibid.: 205–8). But some of the arguments for the differences are phonological in nature, relating specifically to Spanish, as are part of the suggested revised IPA definitions (2004: 208–9), some of which I give below:

j   voiced palatal semi-vowel approximant
w   voiced labial-velar semi-vowel approximant
ɥ   voiced labial-palatal semi-vowel approximant
ɰ   voiced velar semi-vowel approximant
ʋ   voiced labiodental spirant approximant
ɹ   voiced alveolar rhotic approximant
ɻ   voiced retroflex rhotic approximant

'Spirant approximant' is used to differentiate those articulations that do not overlap vocoid ones, for example, [β ð̞ ɣ], which have phonological alternations with the equivalent stops in Spanish. As I have already shown above, there is nothing necessarily phonetic about the phonological functional definitions of consonant, vowel, and semi-vowel; and 'rhotic' is not a phonetic label at all – it's just a fancy term for 'r-like' (see Ladefoged's definition above). And, if that is the case, then in English [ʊ] should also be a 'rhotic'.

The definitions of consonant and vowel may be augmented in language-specific, but functional ways, as we saw in relation to English /h/ and the French approximants. (We should also note that if we accept a non-segmental view of phonology, then the terms consonant and vowel may be epiphenomenal.)

5.9 COMPLEX PHONOLOGICAL FEATURES

In the (non-Firthian) literature on phonology there are a few occasions where a different view of phonological features is entertained. For instance, Blevins (1995: 208) refers to 'ballisticity' as a phonological feature of Otomanguean Amuzgo and Chinantecan. The term refers to a cluster of regularly recurring phonetic features, including fortis initial Cs, voiceless nuclear Vs, final voiceless sonorants, syllable-final aspiration, which Blevins groups together as 'aspiration'; rapid crescendo to peak intensity, with sudden decrescendo; accentuation of vowel length contrasts; tonal gliding; tongue root retraction. Non-ballistic syllables are 'unaspirated', show even rises and falls of intensity, have unexaggerated vowel length contrasts, do not show tonal gliding, and have no tongue root retraction. (I am not in a position to question or verify such descriptions, as I know no native speakers; for me this is a case of library phonology on my part.) This seems entirely parallel to [ATR] in Kalenjin, as discussed in detail in Local & Lodge (1996, 2004). In the Kalenjin dialect of Tugen there is a harmony system that is typically related to the feature [ATR] in the vowels (Hall et al., 1974; Halle & Vergnaud, 1981; Ringen, 1988). Local & Lodge show that in fact the system is based on far more features than a putative advancement of the tongue root. Table 5.1 below gives a summary of these features; see also Local & Lodge (2004: 12). It is interesting to note that, just like [tense] above, [ATR] has proved to be another convenient feature for relating vowel sets, and indeed, since it, too, as a universal feature, has to appear in all languages, it has replaced [tense] in some analyses of systems like English and German (see, for example, Kenstowicz, 1994 and Wiese, 1996). This has happened in spite of the fact that early investigations of the phenomenon in physiological terms

Table 5.1   Summary of features of the harmony system in Kalenjin

[+ATR]	[−ATR]
relatively higher and more peripheral tongue position for vowels	relatively lower and less peripheral tongue position for vowels
relatively shorter consonantal portions, with 'clear' resonance, and longer vocalic portions	relatively longer consonantal portions, with 'dark' resonance, and shorter vocalic portions
final voicelessness in coda approximants	final breathy voice in the rhyme
range of intervocalic consonantal articulations from stop to fricative	range of intervocalic consonantal articulations from fricative to approximant
stability in place of articulation for 'coronals'	variability in place of articulation for 'coronals' (dental or alveolar)

produced only tentative results and suggestions that certainly it was not phonological in languages like English and German, where the advancement of the tongue root was seen as a concomitant movement related to fronting the tongue body (see, for example, Lindau, Jacobson & Ladefoged, 1973).

Both ballisticity and ATR are convenient labels for a complex set of distinctive phonetic features spread throughout the syllable. Such phonetic exponency of these phonological features is unlikely to be universally applicable. The study of phenomena like 'ballisticity' and their phonetic implementation is a step in the right direction with regard to the clear separation of phonetics and phonology.

At this point it would be useful to look at the way in which [ATR] evolved as a phonological feature. It is quite clear that in a number of languages there are harmony systems which are of central phonological importance, as we saw in section 5.4. All of them involve two sets of realizations which alternate in some way, though not always in the same way across languages. Let us call these sets A and B; thus far there can be little disagreement. In the case of [ATR], however, a search has been made for a common denominator of the realization of these sets by investigating some, but not all such languages. This search has been limited from the outset by the unwarranted assumption that the system resided solely in the vowel systems – no doubt to some extent a case of segmental phonology driving the phonetics in a segmental direction. (In Igbo, for instance, there is evidence that coda consonant realizations vary according to the preceding vowel type; see Kelly & Local, 1989: 180.)

The research carried out by Stewart (1967), Lindau (1975, 1978), Ladefoged (1968, 1971, 1972) and Lindau, Jacobson & Ladefoged (1973) establishes a connection between the vowel qualities in the two sets and the position of the tongue root. Lindau, Jacobson & Ladefoged (1973) show that advancing of the tongue root may also be used as a mechanism to alter tongue height, as in German and some English speakers, without there being any justification for giving the mechanism phonological status (see 1973: 87); they thus distinguish between those languages which use tongue root position as the basis of a phonological vowel harmony system and those that use it as an articulatory mechanism for raising the tongue body. Lindau (1978) suggests that the important effect of advancing or retracting the tongue root in general is to change the shape of the pharyngeal opening and labels the phenomenon [Expanded]. This is an elaboration of Ladefoged's (1971, 1972) suggestion that there is a phonological feature Wide covering three states of the pharynx: wide, as in advanced tongue root articulations; neutral, where the tongue root is in its 'normal' position (which may or may not be the position for [−ATR], depending on the language); and narrow, where the tongue root is retracted. The last state may be the equivalent of [−ATR], but Ladefoged exemplifies it with Arabic [ʕ]; Lindau (1978: 553) also suggests that neutral versus narrow is employed in Arabic to differentiate between non-emphatic and emphatic consonants respectively. This is the only reference to consonants in relation to the position of the tongue root.

With the basic groundwork set up in this way it is easy to see how phonologists (who have not necessarily investigated the so-called [ATR] languages directly) find such a feature definition attractive as a generic binary label for the two sets A and B. There is, apparently, a simple phonetic interpretation of the phonological phenomenon, a convenient isomorphism: an advanced tongue root produces a wide pharynx, which equates with [+ATR] in the phonology. Whether [−ATR] is equivalent to a neutral or retracted tongue root is not a question I want to take further here, but the issue has led to the introduction of another feature [RTR] in the analysis of some languages; see Carr, 1993b and refs; see also section 5.4 above.)

Since we are dealing with articulatory gestures which clearly affect consonantal quality, we might be tempted to extend the Ladefoged/ Lindau proposal to any appropriate consonants, as they do for

Arabic. We could then simply say that in Tugen the whole syllable is [±ATR] covering both consonants and vowels.

But if we return to our phonetic investigations, we are then obliged to ask how we can interpret such a feature opposition in terms of our results. Given the realizational details in Table 5.1 above, it is difficult to see the relationship between tongue root position and some of the other articulations involved in sets A and B in the Tugen data we have observed.

I shall consider now a matter that concerns the phonetic implementation of only the vocalic part of the syllable: namely, the realizations of the low vowels. First of all, it is striking to note that in the investigations of those languages which have a low vowel distinction in sets A and B – for example, Akan, (see, for instance, Lindau, 1975, 1978, Lindau, Jacobson & Ladefoged, 1973) – little is said about their qualities, the non-low vowels being the focus of attention. The pharyngeal cross-sections for the latter show clear distinctions in the position of the tongue root, but there are no such cross-sections for the low vowels, transcribed in Lindau (1975) as [ɜ] for [+ATR] and [a] for [−ATR], but in Lindau (1978) as [a] and [ʌ], respectively, without any comment, though on the formant chart (Fig. 7, Lindau, 1978: 552) [a] appears in a relatively back position near to [ɔ], [ʌ] being omitted. In their transcription of Kalenjin Halle & Vergnaud (1981) use [a] and [ɑ], respectively, again without elaboration (unfortunately misinterpreted by Carr, 1993a: 260–2, as [a] and [ɑ], respectively). The important point about the Tugen realizations of the two harmonic sets, as far as the low vowels are concerned, is that we find the counter-intuitive realizations of [ɑ] for [+ATR] and [a] for [−ATR] (cf. the relatively narrow transcriptions in Local & Lodge, 2004). In other words the expected movement of the tongue body on the front–back axis in relation to the assumed position of the tongue root does not occur. Whatever the facts of Akan, in Tugen the tongue body position is clearly not determined by the size of the pharynx, so, even if we restricted the phonological domain of the harmony system to the vowels, for the low vowels we would need the contrary interpretation of [±ATR] to their interpretation for the non-low vowels – not a happy conclusion for universals of phonetic implementation.

As far as consonantal articulations are concerned, we are not given any indication of what happens to them when the pharynx is wide (see, for example, Ladefoged, 1972, or Lindau, 1978). A narrow pharynx, as we have already noted, is used in the production of Arabic emphatic consonants. This is of no help in explaining the consonantal articulations we have observed in Tugen, nor in explaining the difference in phonation types. It is Stewart (1967: 199) who assumes a relationship between [+ATR] and breathy voice, for which we find no evidence; on the contrary, in our data breathy voice in the sonorants goes with the [−ATR] syllables. Similarly, the lenition phenomena and the length phenomena referred to in Table 5.1 and discussed in detail in Local & Lodge (2004) seem to have no connection with pharynx width, any more than the fact that /t/ with [+ATR] is exclusively alveolar, whereas with [−ATR] it varies between alveolar and dental. The only conclusion that can be drawn is that [ATR] can have no 'basic' phonetic interpretation that will allow us to apply it in any meaningful way to the Tugen material under discussion here, and also encompass the other realizations usually associated with [ATR] in other languages.

We, therefore, need to return to our initial labels A and B. As cover terms for the forms that enter into the phonological system, they are as good as anything else in that they are abstractions from the data without any phonetic content or implication. This is not dissimilar to the much simpler example that relates to the phonological status of the feature *alveolar*, or some binary equivalent feature arrays in the definition of English /t d n/, referred to above in section 5.1.

5.10 BACK TO ABSTRACTNESS

An important point is made by Blevins (1995: 239 fn. 31) in which in the context of discussing the abstract nature of the syllable, which is independent of acoustic and articulatory properties of the vocal apparatus, she refers to Brentari's discussion of the syllable structure of American Sign Language (ASL) (1995: 615–19). If ASL has a phonology, then how can phonological elements be phonetically based? Indeed, the inclusion of Brentari's paper in Goldsmith (1995a) is significant, not only because of the greater understanding of the nature of sign languages generally, but also as a recognition of the truly abstract nature of phonological structure. However, it is hard to see how Blevins can reconcile her astute observation about abstractness in phonology and her discussion of sonority as a crucial factor in determining syllable structure.

Sign languages give an extreme instance of phonological features without phonetic content. However, it is necessary to consider how much abstractness applies to spoken languages. It may not be a

matter of an a priori decision between totally abstract or phonetically based phonological features. It may rather be a matter of the
kind of relationships involved between the phonetic substance and
the linguistic structures it encodes. I would, therefore, like to consider ways in which abstractness may be required by phonological
structure.

Let us return to Fudge's statement regarding phonetic content,
which I repeat here for convenience: 'It is . . . dangerous and misleading to say that either articulatory or auditory features ARE the
phonological elements, unless they correlate so closely that no facts
of language are obscured by treating them as if they were the same'
(1967: 4). This is presumably a reference to any circumstances where
it is not possible to represent input and output by the same set of
phonetically based features. OT goes to great lengths to cling to the
notion of input = output by means of its Faithfulness Constraints
(see Kager, 1999), even though they are, of course, violated in many
cases. Indeed, the notion of identity is central to faithfulness (see, for
example, Pulleyblank, 1997; Kager, 1999; Gussenhoven & Jacobs,
2005). But what kind of identity can this be? We saw in Chapter 1
that the only true identity is identity with the self, 'token identity of
the individual.' In OT, identity is defined theory-internally as having
the same features or structure in both input and output representations. This certainly requires the features of both levels to be the same,
not something that is supported by the evidence being reviewed in
this book.

It is important to question the status of such constraints as universals, if it is the norm for them to be violated. In other words, does it
truly reflect the nature of language to suppose that the ideal situation
is input = output? Such an assumption of sameness of features at both
phonological and phonetic levels seems to hark back to the structuralist era when phonological analyses were based entirely in the phonetics (for example, Hockett, 1955; Bloch & Trager, 1942). There are
cases where a direct correlation causes no great difficulty: single-place
onsets in English consist of stops, fricatives or approximants, and can
be so labelled lexically (if need be) or by implicational conditions that
fill in predictable features. (For a discussion of Declarative Phonology
see below, Chapter 6.) On the other hand, so-called coda contrasts
in English are typically rhymal in nature, since they involve duration
differences in the vocoid of the nucleus as well as vocal cord vibration differences. In this case, a distinction using the labels [±voice]
or some unary equivalent is clearly not a direct description of what is

actually articulated. It is not appropriate to dismiss such phenomena as 'low-level, phonetic detail', since any 'allophonic' variation is part of the linguistic structure and native speakers know where to use it and where not. The cessation of voicing before the release of a stop or the cessation of friction in codas is a specifically English characteristic; (standard) French does not employ it and nor does (standard) German. It is not a 'natural', inevitable phenomenon.

A case where there is an even more complex phonetic realization which does not relate directly to traditional segmental labels is furnished by German rhymal /r/ (see Lodge, 2003a). If German /r/ is classified as a consonant, as in Kohler (1977: 159) or Fox (1990: 55–6), then how are we to handle realizations such as those in (5.17)?

(5.17) [ɜʌnˠtˠə]   Ernte 'harvest'
        [vˠɨʀtˠ]   (Es) wird 'it becomes'
        [lˠɛ̈ːnˠtˠ] (Sie) lernt 'she learns'

The solution I propose in Lodge (2003a) is to establish a syllabic or rhymal feature related to pharynx size (the other way of viewing tongue root position, see above) and base the contrast on the normal pharynx size, where there is no '/r/', as in *Ente* 'duck' versus a narrow pharynx with '/r/', as in *Ernte* above. The narrow pharynx also produces the appropriate vocoid differences such as 'r'-less [ɛ ɪ ʊ] and their V + 'r' equivalents [ɜ ɨ o]; for some speakers even the back vowels are further back in association with rhymal /r/. In this case there must be language-specific phonetic implementation statements to the effect that [front] + [normal] when short imply retracted tongue body position, that is, [ɪ] for example; when long, front tongue body position, that is, [iː], whereas [front] + [narrow] imply central tongue body position, and so on. (The extent to which the tongue body position is the result of pharynx size needs careful consideration. The tongue is not compressible: this means that a movement of one part of the tongue must be accompanied by the movement of other parts. Cf. the inconsistent use of *(in)compressible* in the quotations given by Archangeli & Pulleyblank, 1994: 174–5.)

This leads us to the question of whether there should be an abstract feature or features in some cases, which then require language-specific phonetic implementation statements. In the case of German /r/ we could view the abstractness in terms of underspecification, that is the phonological structures are not phonetic in that they cannot be seen as 'instructions to articulate'. So a rhyme such as /-art/ (in phonemic terms) would have a representation as in (5.18).

(5.18)

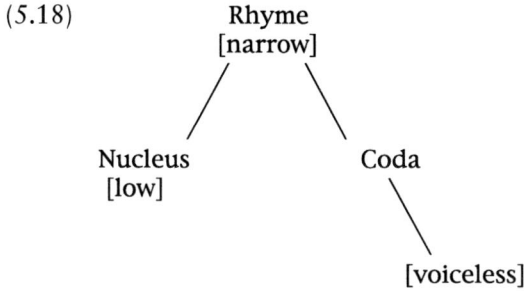

On the other hand, we could establish an abstract phonological feature for German: [± r], which then has its appropriate phonetic implementation. The phonological structure would then be as in (5.19).

(5.19)

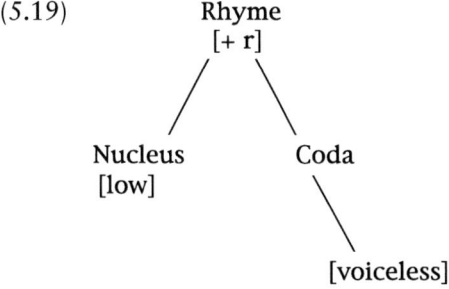

For an approach to phonological structure with abstract phonological elements of this kind, see Ogden (1999); see also Plug & Ogden (2003). For further discussion of such representations of phonological structure, see Chapter 6.

An even more complex case is provided by the Tugen data referred to above. In this case we have claimed it would be very difficult to find some all-embracing feature with phonetic content that could be seen as a trigger for all the characteristics of the harmony sets given in Table 5.1 above. If we want to acknowledge and account for all the patterns of realization involved in the Tugen harmony system, then we are forced to establish an abstract phonological element. If this is what [ATR] means, all well and good, but in practice this is not the way it is viewed, as can be seen from the extensive discussions and references in Archangeli & Pulleyblank (1994). Calling the many harmony systems [ATR]-based systems regardless of how they are realized and then extending the feature to account for very different kinds of distinctions found in English vowels, for example, is certainly a good way of obscuring the facts.

6

DECLARATIVE PHONOLOGY:
AN ALTERNATIVE SET OF PROPOSALS

༄

> There is no time in structure, there is no sequence in structure; time and
> sequence are with reference to the utterance, order and place are with
> reference to structure . . . (Carnochan, *Gemination in Hausa*)

This chapter presents a set of proposals to take account of the views
laid out in the previous chapters. As such, it does not deal with sameness and difference directly, but deals with the relationship between
meaning and sound, that is, between phonological storage and phonetic realization. If the points of view taken in earlier chapters hold
good, then we need to consider the details of this relationship in the
context of a polysystemic, non-segmental, abstract approach of the
kind presented in Lodge (2003a, 2007).

6.1 DERIVATION

Whether or not we decide on a monosystemic or a polysystemic
approach, segments or layers of prosodic features, binary or unary
features, there is a matter which cuts across all these alternatives, the
matter of whether or not we allow processes to apply to our preferred
representations, thereby altering the phonological input in some way
to achieve a representation of the output. (The issue of whether the
output of grammars is actual speech or not has been addressed in
Chapter 5.)

Let us start with the German obstruents that we have already discussed briefly from the point of view of monosystemicity in Chapter
3. We find alternating voiceless and voiced obstruents in many lexical
items. The crucial examples are given in (6.1).

(6.1) [bliːp] *blieb*   [bliːbm] *blieben*, past tense of *bleiben*
   [miːt] *mied*   [miːdn] *mieden*, past tense of *meiden*
   [bliːs] *blies*   [bliːzn] *bliesen*, past tense of *blasen*
   [tsoːk] *zog*   [tsoːgŋ] *zogen*, past tense of *ziehen*

Here we find the stem-final obstruent alternates in each case, so that when it is in final position it is voiceless, otherwise it is voiced. In fact, it is the syllable-final position that is crucial here, and complex forms conform to this generalization, for example, *ableiten* with [ap-]. We saw in Chapter 3 that Chomsky (1964) argued strongly against any interpretation that implied a change of phoneme in such cases. This seems to be the approach suggested by, for example, Fox (1990: 69), as represented in (6.2).

(6.2)   /b/ → /p/
          /d/ → /t/
          /z/ → /s/
          /g/ → /k/

Such a solution would involve an inordinate number of morphophonemic rules and assumes the extreme form of biuniqueness we rejected in Chapter 3. But since there is no change of meaning, no change of phoneme needs to be involved, especially if we adhere to the Unique Underlier Condition. An alternative is given in (6.3), where the right-hand symbols represent phonetic realizations, not phonemes.

(6.3)   /b/ → [p]
          /d/ → [t]
          /z/ → [s]
          /g/ → [k]

In a system of SPE-style binary features these instances can all be treated by a rule such as (6.4).

(6.4)   [+voi] → [−voi]

It is clear that on uttering [t] or [s] in such circumstances, a speaker cannot start out with voicing and alter it to voicelessness, and that we are dealing with a metaphorical process of change in such a representation, a way of relating lexical forms to a representation of (an approximation of) what speakers actually produce. But the metaphor is a powerful one and can lead to unfounded claims of the kind we considered in section 5.3, such that any phonetic form [A] can turn into another phonetic form [B]. In this case at the underlying, lexical level all these alternating morphemes end in a voiced obstruent, for example, /bli:b/, /mi:d/, /bli:z/, /tso:g/, to which the process in (6.4) applies in syllable-final position.

The process interpretation assumes that the underlying specification of the voiced obstruents is something like that in (6.5).

(6.5)

/b/	/d/	/g/	/z/
[+ant]	[+ant]	[−ant]	[+ant]
[−cor]	[+cor]	[−cor]	[+cor]
[+voi]	[+voi]	[+voi]	[+voi]
[−cont]	[−cont]	[−cont]	[+cont]
[−son]	[−son]	[−son]	[−son]

The rule will then pick out the voiced obstruents from all other phonemes of German and state that they must be [−voi] in syllable-final position. Thus our informal presentation in (6.4) will be formalized as in (6.6) (taken from Brockhaus, 1990: 271, with the environment changed from word-boundary (#) to syllable-boundary ($)).

(6.6)   [−son] → [−voi] / ____$

Hence all [+voi] specifications in (6.5) and any other obstruents will be changed in the appropriate circumstances. Such feature-changing rules are required only because of the assumption that all phonological representations have to be fully specified with features having some form of direct phonetic interpretation. Hence metaphors of change are invoked: X becomes Y. (See also Fudge's, 1967, reservations discussed in section 5.2 above.)

The alternative to such an interpretation of the alternation is to avoid any kind of process mechanism. If we say that such alternating morphemes in German have final consonants that are neither voiced nor voiceless then we can state the conditions under which each alternant occurs without any recourse to changing one feature into another. This is the basis of underspecification, which is a requirement of a non-derivational, declarative account of phonological structure. I shall return to this alternative view of phonological structure in the next section.

As long ago as 1954 Hockett was concerned with the difference in interpretation of morphological alternations as procedure or state. He characterized two different views of linguistic structure as item and arrangement (IA) and item and process (IP). He was not questioning the interpretation of 'item' as being anything other than a segment but was asking, rather, what to do with that item when we describe certain phenomena that involve alternative realizations. IA made non-procedural statements about the relationships between morphemes, whereas the IP approach saw morphological relationships as the result of morphemes undergoing a process of change, /A/ → /B/ (cf. Hockett, 1954: 229–30).

Of course, Hockett was discussing morphology rather than phonology, but the same principles apply and it is this basic IP approach
that was taken over by the generative interpretation of linguistic
structure. It suited the purpose of meeting the unique underlier condition (discussed above in section 3.4 and in Lass, 1984: 63, 203–35)
that requires each morpheme to have a single form for storage in the
lexicon. All alternative realizations are then derived from that single
form. The concept of derivation is central to all classical generative
phonology, as enshrined in Chomsky & Halle (1968). There are
still staunch supporters of derivation in phonology (for example,
Bromberger & Halle, 1989 & 1997; Iverson, 1995), though there
have also been many critics (see Durand & Katamba, 1995, and some
of the contributions in Roca, 1997).

The main criticism of derivation and feature-changing rules is
that, as a means of mapping underlying lexical forms to their surface
realizations, they are far too powerful for an appropriate theory
of language. Let us take a fairly extreme example from English, as
analyzed by Chomsky & Halle (1968). The morpheme *right* does
not undergo trisyllabic laxing (Chomsky & Halle, 1968: 180, 241)
of the kind found in the Latinate vocabulary of English, as in *divine*
– *divinity*. *Right* maintains its long vowel [aɪ] even in derived forms,
for example, *righteous* [raɪtʃəs]. In order to stop the rule of trisyllabic laxing from applying, thereby producing *[rɪʃəs], Chomsky
& Halle propose an underlying form of *right* which has a voiceless
velar fricative as the penultimate consonant: /rixt/ (cf. 1968: 233–4,
for a discussion and the rather complex derivation that is entailed
by their analysis). The choice of /x/ as the underlying consonant can
only be justified in historical terms; in Middle English (most) words
spelt today with *gh* had a velar fricative. There is no evidence from
Modern English (American or British) to support such a choice.
(Note that some dialects of English, for instance, broad Scots, cf.
Wells, 1982, still retain the fricative in such words, but knowledge of
all dialects of English is not something that native speakers have, a
point we shall elaborate in the next chapter; cf. Trudgill, 1983. Note,
also, that at the time when standardization of the spelling system was
taking place, a time much closer to Middle English than today, but
when the standardized dialect had nevertheless lost the earlier velar
fricative, those responsible for the spelling system were not aware
of the actual occurrence of historical /x/, so that they spelt *delight*
with *gh*, even though it came from Old French *delite* and is related
to *delicious*.) In addition to the somewhat arbitrary choice of a velar

fricative to save *right* from trisyllabic laxing, there is the question as to how widespread this phoneme is in English. True, Chomsky & Halle (1968: 234) use it as the underlier of [h], but this is merely a way of using it further once it has been established. In fact, *right* is the only word that behaves like this, that is to say, it is highly exceptional. The two other morphemes that Chomsky and Halle suggest contain /x/ are *nightingale* and *might*. The former does not enter into any alternations (even if *night-* could be identified as the same as *night* – but what on earth is *-ingale*?) and so the first syllable can be represented as /nīt-/ underlyingly (in SPE terms), which will predict the right surface form without any extra processes. The set of forms *might–mighty–mightily* are exactly parallel to sets like *(sp)ice–(sp) icy–(sp)icily* and *slime–slimy–slimily*, which have never had a velar fricative in their earlier forms. Such sets suggest that it is only certain disyllabic endings that trigger trisyllabic laxing, further evidence that this is not a general phonological process in English but one that is lexically restricted, occurring only in certain types of word, mainly Latinate ones. (See Lodge, 1986, for a discussion of the English velar fricative in the framework of Dependency Phonology.)

A consequence of the concept of derivation in combination with monosystemicity and biuniqueness (see Chapter 3) is the 'free-ride principle'. To return to our English example of trisyllabic laxing, there are many morphemes with alternating stem vowels that have been borrowed from Latin, as in (6.7).

(6.7) divine   divinity
       serene   serenity
       sane   sanity
       profound   profundity
       verbose   verbosity

However, there are also forms with the long vowels represented on the left which do not enter into any alternations, for example, *size*, *meat*, *save*, *blouse*, *stone*. According to the free-ride principle such words have the same vowel phonemes in the lexicon as those that alternate, and enjoy a 'free ride' through the same derivation, that is, they are not affected by some or any of the feature-changing rules.

One could propose that morphemes that have alternative realizations should be marked as different in the lexicon from those that do not – after all, it is part of native speaker knowledge to know this difference. On this basis morphemes like *serene* would be given a stressed vowel /ē/ (using the SPE symbols), whereas *meat* would be given, say, /iː/. Exceptional Latinate forms, which do not undergo tri-syllabic laxing, for example, *obese – obesity*, can also be represented with the non-alternating /iː/, which is not subject to the rule. This proposal would be perfectly feasible if we abandon biuniqueness, but would entail an element of polysystemicity not found in generative phonology.

Another issue concerning derivation is the assumed centrality of the citation form. This affects the interpretation of alternate realiza-tions of a lexical item rather than morphophonological alternations. In the case of the latter in German, for instance, the citation form would have the voiceless obstruent in nouns and adjectives, for example, *Bund, brav, Krieg*, whereas morphologically complex forms such as the verbs, which conventionally use the infinitive form for citation, contain the voiced realization, for example, *bleiben*. And in any case, bound morphemes do not have citation forms, which are generally speaking understood as the word (simple or complex) said in isolation, as presented in dictionaries, for example. So, citation forms relate to the range of realizations of individual lexical items and are interpreted as a base form from which alternative realiza-tions are derived (cf. Lass, 1984: 30, 295–8), but the citation form is not always the base form, as we can see from the German nouns above. What is of concern to anyone who takes actual speech as the data to be accounted for by phonology (for example, Docherty & Foulkes, 2000) is that the utterances native speakers produce, vari-able though they are, are the more common forms that speakers use and hear, not the citation forms. It is true that in order to account for the relatedness of diverse phonetic realizations of the lexical items we need some kind of phonological form, but the citation form is not necessarily the best starting point. Certainly, if we do take the citation form as a starting point, then we need a large number of derivational rules, some of which will be highly restricted in their generality. The same point could be made in relation to child utterances of the kind we discussed in section 4.3 above; a segment-by-segment account of the kind proposed, for example, by Smith (1973) would involve a number of *ad hoc* rules for what can be interpreted quite easily as a matter of timing differences *vis-à-vis* adult articulations of the same phonological sequence.

But, throughout the book so far, the application of the require-ments of segmentation, biuniqueness and monosystemicity have been shown to have inappropriate consequences for the purposes of estab-lishing a phonology based on the principles of functional sameness and difference. And one of those consequences is the requirement to incorporate derivational machinery into the grammar.

6.2 DECLARATIVE PHONOLOGY

The extreme alternative position to accepting derivation as a legitimate means of representing the relationship between phonological and phonetic forms is one which excludes any kind of feature-changing or feature-removal from the outset. A move to reject derivational approaches as too powerful gained momentum in the 1990s (see, for example, the debate in Durand & Katamba, 1995), resulting in GP (Kaye, Lowenstamm & Vergnaud, 1985, Charette, 1991), OT (Kager, 1999, Archangeli & Langendoen, 1997) and Declarative Phonology (Bird, 1995, Ogden, 1999, Lodge, 2003a, 2007), all of which claim to be process free. Basically, constraints take over the derivational processing of underlying forms. If phonological theory involves no feature-changing or structure-destroying processes and is hence non-derivational, then the phonological storage forms will have to be underspecified or completely abstract, that is, without any phonetic content. Any statements regarding legitimate structures are constraints on possible linguistic forms; such constraints may be either negative or positive in nature (see the discussion in Hale & Reiss, 2000, on this point). It is also the case that constraints may be seen as being violable, as in OT, for example, or inviolable, as in Declarative Phonology. Constraint violability goes along with allowing only universal constraints, which are violable according to a language-specific hierarchical ranking (OT); constraint inviolability allows no violation of any constraints, whether universal or local.

If we wish to exclude derivational processes from our grammars and yet give alternant realizations of morphemes a single lexical phonological representation, then underspecification of the feature(s) involved in the alternations is a necessary consequence. It is only if we insist on fully specified lexical entry forms that we need derivational machinery and/or a set of morphophonemic statements.

It is now appropriate to provide an outline of Declarative Phonology in order to see how it deals with some of the issues I have pinpointed as problems with other approaches. This presentation is based on Bird (1995), Scobbie, Bird & Coleman (1996), Scobbie (1997), Ogden (1999) and Lodge (2003a, 2007). Phonological structure is represented in terms of attribute-value matrices (AVMs) of the kind proposed by Bird (1995) and Ogden (1999), where the value can itself be an AVM and where the feature structure can consist of more than one attribute-value pair, as in (6.8) from Ogden (1999).

(6.8)

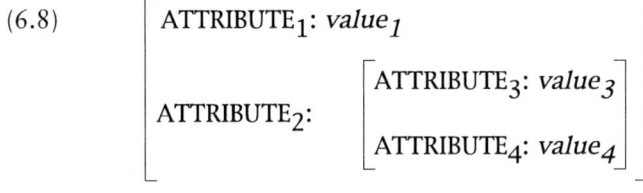

Attributes are written in capitals and the values in italics where they refer to types, such as *onset* or *rhyme*. The subscript indices ensure that attributes and values are paired appropriately; for instance, the value of ONSET must be of the type *onset* and not *rhyme*, etc.

What constitutes an attribute and what a value depends on the particular view of feature arrays in phonological representations. Bird (1995) and Ogden (1999) use binary features in the manner of SPE so that the attribute is a feature and the value is plus or minus, as in (6.9) which represents [voiced].

(6.9)   [VOICE: +]

Lodge (2003a), on the other hand, uses a layered approach to structure (see also Lodge, 1992, 1993, 1995) with unary features relating to each layer. In this case the attribute is a layer and the value one of a set of unary features exclusively associated with that layer, as in (6.10).

(6.10)   [PHONATION: voiced]

Lexical entry forms are highly underspecified: only those features needed to differentiate each contrastive structure from every other in the system are entered. Some features are universally unspecified, others on a language-specific basis. For example, stops are the universally unmarked manner of articulation (see Stemberger, 1991) and coronality is the default place of articulation (see Paradis & Prunet, 1991), so it is not usually specified (on French coronals, however, see Lodge, 2005: 248–51). This means that in systems with /t/, /d/ and /n/ none of them will be specified for these two features. The other crucial factor in determining which features are unspecified is the matter of alternant realizations. Any underlying phonological unit that has a range of realizations will have to be unspecified for the relevant feature(s) if we are to avoid any feature-changing and deletion mechanisms, as already pointed out above. So, in cases where obligatory (or even optional, see Lodge, 1992) assimilation takes place, as in the case of Modern Greek onset stops, which are voiceless in all cases except after the lexical /n/ of a number of function words such as the definite article and the negative particle, then the phonation feature cannot be specified (see Lodge, 2005: 242–8 for a treatment of this and related phenomena in Greek). In place of derivational rules, what we have in a declarative approach are sets of statements that fill in the unspecified features. This occurs in two ways: predictive statements and default statements (cf. also Wiese, 1996: 150–77). I choose the term 'statement' rather than 'rule' so that there is no suggestion of any processes implicit in the latter term, given its use in derivational phonology. I will return to the nature of these statements after introducing the representational feature system.

I am assuming that, rather than is the case in segment-based approaches, phonological structure is layered as in Firthian prosodic analysis (Firth, 1948; Palmer, 1970) and in a way similar to other 'non-linear' approaches (Clements and Hume, 1995; Kaye, Lowenstamm & Vergnaud, 1985). In addition, however, there is an anisomorphism between syllable places and phonetic features, so that features may be attached to any syllable node, not just terminal nodes, or even at levels higher than the syllable, if necessary, such as in the case of English /l/ and /r/, discussed in section 4.2 above, where the resonance features are often foot-length. As I point out in Lodge (2003a), German rhymal /r/ is a good example of this anisomorphism in that some of its realizational features are syllable length. On this basis the structure of rhymes with codas can be represented as in (6.11).

(6.11)

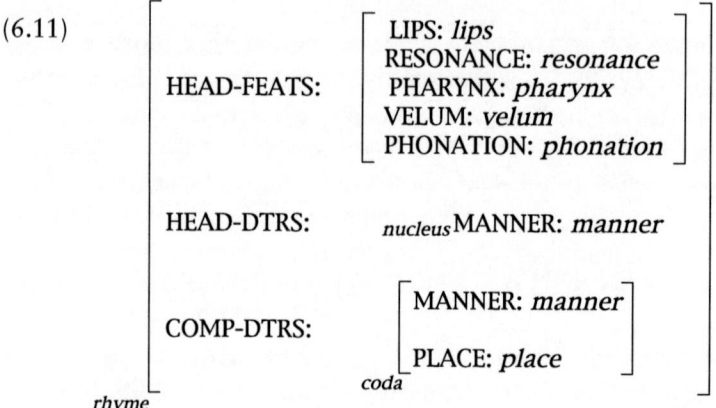

This means that some of the features are rhymal, for example, those of the lips and resonance (though, in fact, as I point out in Lodge,

2003a, with reference to German /r/, they are typically syllabic), whereas others are associated with the coda syllable node(s) only, for example, manner and place features.

Each of the layers represents a set of phonetically-based features, such as those given in (6.12), as an expansion of each italicized value in (6.11) (see Lodge, 1992, 1993, 1995).

(6.12)

> *lips:* {spread, neutral, round}
> *resonance:* {front, retracted, central, advanced, back}
> *pharynx:* {wide, normal, narrow}
> *velum:* {oral, nasal}
> *phonation:* {voiced, voiceless}
> $_{nucleus}$ *manner:* {high, mid, low}
> *manner:* {stop, fricative, lateral, trill, approximant, high, mid, low}
> *place:* {bilabial, labiodental, alveolar, palato-alveolar, dorsal, uvular}

Note that, as indicated in (6.10) above, the attribute is the layer and the value is one of the possible unary features.

The abstract nature of phonology that is a characteristic of Declarative Phonology (see Bird, 1995 and Ogden, 1999) is handled in my approach by having highly underspecified lexical entry forms, which are combined with other forms and/or built up by implicational statements relating predictable features to the lexically given ones. The lexically specified features are the lowest common denominators of the possible realizations. It is, of course, possible to require totally abstract phonological entities, as in a Firthian approach, which are then interpreted phonetically in ways appropriate to each language (cf. Ogden, 1999; compare (5.18) and (5.19) above as alternative representations of rhymal /r/ in German). In this presentation I have chosen a more direct form of phonetic interpretation of the features in most cases, though it is clear that further interpretative statements are needed in several cases, for example in so-called ATR-harmony systems (see Local & Lodge, 1996, 2004), where [ATR] could be seen as an abstract phonological feature to be interpreted in accordance with fairly widespread phonetic features, as presented in Table 5.1 above, and in the case of vowel quality in German with and without rhymal /r/ (Lodge, 2003a). Hence the need for a phonetic implementation component to interpret the features in any representation, whether partly phonetic or totally abstract (see section 6.3).

Syllable structure is based on the principle of headedness (as in Dependency Phonology, Anderson & Ewen, 1987) with a general representation as in (6.13), from Ogden (1999: 61).

(6.13)   syllable (σ)

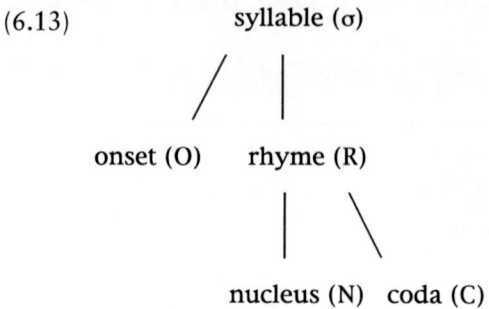

onset (O)   rhyme (R)

nucleus (N)   coda (C)

As already established above, features can attach to any of these nodes. Phonological structure can be represented either as AVMs, as in (6.11) and in (6.22) below, or as partially specified trees in the form of (6.13) or of (5.18) and (5.19) above. In what follows I shall mostly use the latter for simplicity of presentation.

Lexical entries are highly underspecified in order to avoid all destructive and feature-changing operations. To provide the other features we need sets of statements that specify the co-occurrence of features; these are either predictive, as in (6.14) or default, as in (6.15), where F = any feature, L = the appropriate layer, and the arrow is an *if/then* implication.

(6.14) $F_i \rightarrow F_j$
(6.15) $L \rightarrow F_i$

(6.15) is to be read as 'If layer L is unspecified, then F_i is the default feature.' The statements, which can also be interpreted as constraints on structure, are subdivided into context-specific groups, that is, those that relate to the rhyme, the onset, the nucleus, the coda and so on. There are a number of universal default statements that apply to articulations generally, as in (6.16), that we referred to above.

(6.16)

  (a) PLACE → [alveolar]
  (b) MANNER → [stop]
  (c) VELUM → [oral]

(Formulated in this way, the constraints are positive statements, that is, they state what is permissible, as opposed to stating what is not; see the discussion in Hale & Reiss, 2000.)

Predictive statements may be universal or language-specific. The fact that all languages have at least some back rounded vowels would be accounted for by (6.17), and (6.18) would apply to those languages with the fricatives [f v ʃ ʒ], such as English, French and German.

(6.17)   [round] → [back]

(6.18) $\left\{ \begin{array}{l} \text{[labiodental]} \\ \\ \text{[palato-alveolar]} \end{array} \right\}$ → [fricative]

The universal implication given in (6.19) using SPE binary features does not have an exact equivalent in this approach.

(6.19)   [αson] → [αvoi]

Firstly, there is no formal equivalent of the dichotomy obstruent versus sonorant ([±son]) given the feature set *manner* in (6.12). Secondly, it may be necessary in some languages to specify obstruents lexically as [voiceless] rather than by default. That sonorants are typically voiced can be covered by the statement (6.20).

(6.20)   PHONATION → [voiced]

The part of (6.19) relating to obstruents could be represented by the less elegant (6.21).

(6.21)
MANNER → $\left\{ \begin{array}{l} \text{[fricative]} \\ \\ \text{[stop]} \end{array} \right\}$
PHONATION → [voiceless]

However, in languages such as German and Russian, which have some version of the Coda Obstruent Phonation (COP) constraint (Final Obstruent Devoicing), the non-alternating voiceless obstruents will be lexically specified as [voiceless], as mentioned above. The COP will then be a structural requirement on codas, as in (6.22) (cf. Lodge, 2003a).

(6.22)
$$\begin{bmatrix} \text{COMP-DTRS:} & \begin{bmatrix} \text{[VELUM: oral]} \\ \text{[PHONATION: voiceless]} \\ \begin{bmatrix} \text{MANNER:} & \left\{ \begin{array}{l} \text{fricative} \\ \text{stop} \end{array} \right\} \end{bmatrix}_{coda} \end{bmatrix} \end{bmatrix}_{rhyme}$$

The alternating obstruents are subject to (6.20) when they are ambisyllabic and (6.22) in the coda; the non-alternating obstruents, which are specified as [voiceless] lexically, conform to (6.22) in any case.

Despite the fact that there are lexically specified features and predicted and default features are added to these, there is no derivational procedure. Rather than as in earlier versions of underspecification theory – for example, Archangeli (1984, 1988); Pulleyblank (1988a, b) – which were still allied to derivations with the filling-in of unspecified features occurring at various stages in the derivation, underspecification resides strictly in the lexical storage forms only, and all filling-in statements apply at once. If this were not the case, derivation would creep back in. Rule ordering is not an issue. If there are optional realizations of the phonological structure, as in the case of place assimilations in English, then any set of filled-in features appropriate to the circumstances will apply. (This mechanism can be refined as we get to understand the circumstances in which the alternant realizations occur, which may well be sociolinguistic in nature as well as phonological, or discourse-related.)

In Lodge (2005: 242) I refer to spreading in relation to assimilation. Since this term has a suggestion of a process and hence of derivation, it should be reformulated in such a way that it is clear that the concept within Declarative Phonology is not intended to be an illicit process smuggled in by the back door. In Lodge (2005) spreading was conceived of as a mechanism that simply added feature specifications where there are none, for example, after morpheme concatenation, but it did not involve the destructive process of delinking, thereby employing feature changing. However, even in the case of optional assimilation, there is no need to propose even a general statement of filling in any still unspecified features. The extent of a particular feature can be accounted for by differential attachment to the syllable nodes. In the case of Modern Greek, where assimilation of place and voice is obligatory in certain circumstances (for details, see Lodge, 2005: 242–8), place features are attached at an ambisyllabic consonant level (coda/onset) at the word boundaries in question, which correctly specifies the place in all cases. In English, on the other hand, where inter-word place assimilation in cases like *ten men*, *good boy* and *bent girder* is optional, the choice is between (at least) coda/onset feature attachment or just onset attachment with the coda unspecified, so that the default statement (6.16a) applies.

In the case of preaspirated coda stops in Icelandic, where the vocoid features of the nucleus occur automatically in the first coda slot, the representation in (6.23) (as Lodge, 2007: 98 (26)) can be reformulated as (6.24) with all the relevant features attached to the rhymal node.

(6.23)

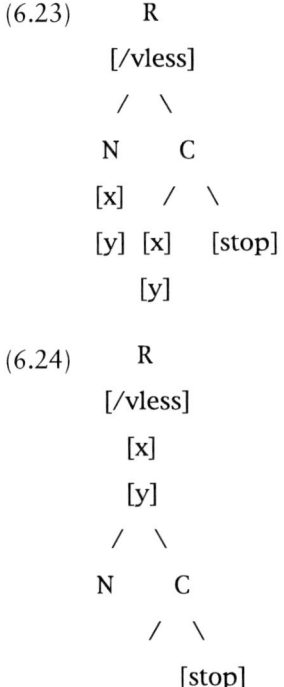

(6.24)   R

    [/vless]

     [x]

     [y]

   / \

  N   C

     / \

      [stop]

6.3 PHONETIC IMPLEMENTATION

Having established a system of representation of phonological structure, we now have to consider how instances of such structure are
interpreted phonetically. Rather than assuming some kind of intrinsic
phonetic interpretation, as discussed in Chapter 5 in particular, the
phonology must have a subcomponent that tells us how native speakers implement the structures of its lexical items, preferably when con-
catenated into an utterance. That this cannot be done one word at a
time should be obvious from the interrelatedness of items in any utterance. The phonetic exponency of any particular structure will need
specific (not universal) presentation in the grammar. Such statements
of implementation will give detailed descriptions of the articulation
and/or acoustics involved for any feature or constellation of features.
Although [bilabial] may have a straightforward interpretation in many
circumstances as 'involves an approximation of both lips', or some such
articulatory instruction, there are many other details – for example,
relative duration of particular articulations – that need to be clearly
spelt out. The kind of variable interpretation of a feature is exemplified
by Lodge (2007: 98–9). In Icelandic, as we saw in section 4.5, some

nuclei have a final voiceless phase, in others not. This is reflected by the attachment of [voiceless] to the rhymal node or the coda node, respectively. Rhymal [voiceless] is implemented as in (6.25).

(6.25) $_{rhyme}$[voiceless] = voice offset time occurs during the nucleus at between X% and Y% of the duration of the vocoid articulation and continues through the coda

Given the variability of realization even in one and the same speaker, it is not meaningful to give precise figures for the onset and offset points of voicing, though the percentages could be replaced by milliseconds in cases where a number of measurements were made of actual speakers. It must also be pointed out that some speakers of Icelandic use a combination of breathy voice, friction and voicelessness as the phonetic exponents of preaspiration (cf. Helgason, 2002: 52 and Lodge, 2007: 93), which would make the implementation statements more complicated, but necessary to capture the habits of those speakers. Coda [voiceless], on the other hand, where preaspiration is not involved, will be implemented as in (6.26).

(6.26) $_{coda}$[voiceless] = voice offset time occurs at the end of the vocoid articulation and continues through any contoid constriction (and any release phase in the case of stops)

The duration of any articulation is also handled in the phonetic implementation component. In the case of languages which have onset voiceless aspirated stops (English, German, Icelandic, Mandarin Chinese, Thai) the voice onset time will be specified in a statement such as (6.27).

(6.27) $_{onset}$[voiceless] = voice onset time occurs during the following nucleus at between X% and Y% of the duration of the vocoid articulation

What is unnecessary, if we get the details of these implementation statements right, is the interpolation of a surface phonetic structure as assumed by most current theories, between the phonological storage forms and actual speech. Phonetic structure in such approaches still has to be implemented in articulatory and acoustic terms, and I have tried to show that reliance on an intrinsic interpretation is insufficient. A direct phonetic interpretation of the phonological structure of the kind I propose here obviates the need for the extra structural level. The alternation of vowel duration in Icelandic is dealt with as a matter of contextually determined phonetic realizations and does not have to be represented at the syllabic or any other level. And the same applies to pre- and postaspiration, provided we assume underspecified phonological forms of the kind proposed in the previous section.

6.4 SOME EXAMPLES

I shall now consider the representation in Declarative Phonology terms of some of the analyses I have already introduced in the preceding chapters, and elaborate on them further, if necessary.

6.4.1 Syllable level attachment in Irish and Malay

Of the suggested set of phonological features given in (6.12) above some of them are attached typically at one particular level, though such attachment is not necessarily to be interpreted as universal. For instance, resonance and lip-position features are often attached at syllable level. Some of the examples of resonance in Irish that were presented in section 4.6 would have attachment at this level, as in (6.28) and (6.29). Whether these are lexical attachments, predictive or default, I cannot say without a complete analysis of the resonance system in Irish, but whichever of the three possibilities it is, the attachment would still be at the same level.

(6.28)

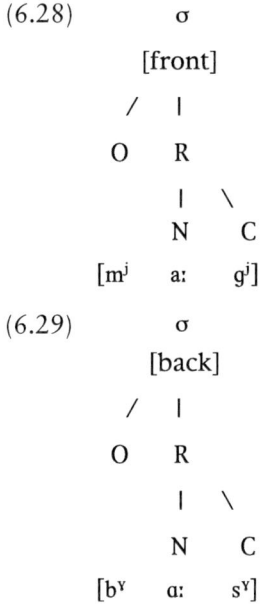

(6.29)

If the resonance changes within the syllable, then the attachment is lower down in the syllable structure, as in (6.30).

(6.30)

```
                σ
          /    |
         O     R
     [front] [back]
                |    \
                N     C
         [ʃ    ɑː    nʸ]
```

The genitive form [ʃaːnʲ] has [front] resonance throughout. In cases where consonantal places have contrasting resonance, the features are attached at place level or higher, as appropriate, as in (6.31) and (6.32).

(6.31)

```
         R
         |  \
         N   C
     [back] [front]
       [ɑː   lʲ]
```

(6.32)

```
         R
       [back]
         |  \
         N   C
       [ɑː   lʸ]
```

In Malay, nasality is a syllable-level and in some cases word-level feature (see Lodge, 1993 for details). The examples in (6.33) show that it is the obstruents and /r/ that inhibit nasality.

(6.33)   [nãnti]   to wait
         [mẽdʒə]   table
         [mãhãl]   expensive
         [mãʔãp]   to forgive
         [gunõŋ]   mountain

So in some cases we have syllable-level attachment, in others it occurs at word level, as in (6.34) and (6.35), respectively.

(6.34)

```
                    W
                 /     \
            σ             σ
                        [nasal]
          /  |         /  |
         O   R        O   R
             |            |  \
             N            N   C
       [g    u        n   õ   ŋ]
```

(6.35)

```
                    W
                 [nasal]
                 /     \
            σ             σ
          /  |         /  |
         O   R        O   R
             |            |  \
             N            N   C
       [m    ã        h̃   ã   ĩ]
```

The default velic feature [oral] is attached at syllable or word level, too.

6.4.2 Feature attachment in German

Similarly, lip-rounding in German would be (at least) syllable length, so we have the partial representations in (6.36) for *Beet* and (6.37) for *Boot*.

(6.36)

```
            σ
        [spread]
        /   |
       O    R
            |  \
            N   C
      [b    eː   t]
```

(6.37)   σ

        [round]

      / |

    O   R

         | \

         N   C

    [b   o: t]

Any umlaut vowels, as in *böte* paired with *bot* (subjunctive II and past tense, respectively, of *bieten* 'to offer') will have [front] added to the nucleus, as in (6.38).

(6.38)   σ

        [round]

      / |

    O   R

         | \

         N   C

        [front]

    [b   ø: t   ə]

In cases such as (6.38), where the lip-rounding changes to neutral during the coda consonant, details of this kind will be spelt out in the phonetic implementation component.

6.4.3 German vowels

At this point I want to present a brief sketch of the German vowel system found in the nominal, adjectival and regular verb word classes. (Note that I have already suggested that more restricted classes, for example, the strong verbs, need separate treatment; see section 3.3 above.) I shall treat the long and short monophthongal pairs in the same way, and leave out the diphthongs for the purpose of this exemplification. The distinctive pairs are as in (6.39).

(6.39) [ɪ] sich   [iː] siech
        [ɛ] Bett   [eː] Beet
        [a] satt   [aː] Saat

[Y]	füllen	[y:]	fühlen
[œ]	Hölle	[ø:]	Föhn
[ʊ]	muß	[u:]	Mus
[ɔ]	Botte	[o:]	Bote

The front rounded vowels in the above examples are not in an umlaut relationship, so need to be differentiated from those that are. The pairs that are not front and rounded, which I will symbolize mnemonically I E A O U, have the lexical representations shown in (6.40). The features are represented on their respective, separate layers

(6.40) /I/   /E/   /A/   /O/   /U/

                          [spread] [round]   [round]

        [front]   [front]

                  [low]   [low]

[round] and (default) [spread] are attached at syllable level, as in (6.36) and (6.37) above. The vowels that never enter into umlaut pairs as the non-umlauted member, /i:/, /ɪ/, /e:/ and /ɛ/, are specified as [front], and lexical Œ and Y are also so specified, as in (6.41).

(6.41) /Œ/   /Y/
        [round]   [round]
        [front]   [front]
        [low]

    In those circumstances where umlaut applies the lexical representations will acquire the specification [front], as in the long vowels in (6.42).

(6.42) [e:]   [ø:]   [y:]
        [spread] [round]   [round]
        [front]   [front]   [front]
                  [low]

Note that umlaut [e:] and phonological /e:/ appear to have different specifications, but this is because they are not fully specified in (6.40) and (6.42). Any remaining features of the vowels will be filled in by predictive and default statements to give [central], [back], [high] and [spread] in the appropriate places, as in (6.43), along with (6.17) to predict [back] from [round] (except where umlaut triggers [front]), (6.20) for the specification of phonation and (6.16c) for velic closure.

(6.43)

     (a) $_{nucleus}$MANNER → [high]
     (b) $_{syll}$LIPS → [spread]
     (c) $_{syll}$RESONANCE → [central]
     (d) [spread] → [low]

Note that (6.43c) only applies to lexically specified [spread], that is, A. Only if umlaut does not trigger [front] will [central] be specified; [low] will be specified in either case.

The vowel system is divided into long and short types, the former including the diphthongs. As in English, short vowels must have at least one following coda consonant. In the case of long monophthongs the nucleus is branching, but the features are attached at nucleus level, as opposed to the diphthongs, which have differential features at each node. The details of realization are dealt with in the phonetic implementation component, so the [low], for example, in short vowels will be interpreted as low-mid and retracted, but in a long vowel as high-mid. Vocoid duration varies with contoid duration as between long and short vowels (see Simpson, 1998 for details) and the effects of rhymal /r/ are discussed in Lodge (2003a). A lexical representation of *Tür* 'door', assuming universal defaults of [stop] for manner of articulation and [alveolar] for place in the onset consonant is given in (6.44).

(6.44)   σ

        [round]

        [narrow]

        [front]

      / |

     O   R

[voiceless] | \

        N   C

    [t   yː   ʌ]

The phonetic implementation will then interpret the combinations of features such as [narrow], [front] and vowel length in a way that is consistent with the habits of groups of native speakers. But not one feature is changed or deleted from the lexical representation and features of different extent interact with one another to be interpreted as phonetic parameters of varying duration. For instance, we need a general statement for standard German to the effect that the duration of the hold phase of the initial stop is shorter before a long vowel than before a short vowel.

6.4.4 Lenition in Gaelic

In section 3.2 I presented some of the morphophonological alternations that trigger lenition in Scots Gaelic. I repeat them yet again as (6.45).

(6.45)   Radical consonant: [pʰ tʰ kʰ p t k m f s]
         Lenited equivalent: [f h x v ɣ ɣ v Ø h]

(Both [tʰ] and [s] have [x] as their lenited form in some dialects.) The lexical entry forms of the radicals are given in (6.46) (without resonance features), with the features in abbreviated form.

(6.46)

/pʰ/	/p/	/tʰ/	/t/	/kʰ/	/k/	/m/	/f/	/s/
[vless]		[vless]		[vless]				[vless]
	[oral]		[oral]		[oral]			[oral]
[lab]	[lab]			[dor]	[dor]	[lab]		

Because it alternates with zero, /f/ must be completely unspecified. The redundant, predictable features are provided by predictive and default statements. The ones in (6.47) are triggered by the lenition environments only.

(6.47)

        (a) MANNER → [fric]
        (b) PLACE → [dor]
        (c) VELUM → [oral]

(6.47a) specifies the friction in lenited forms, (6.47b) the dorsality of /t/, and (6.47c) ensures no nasality in the lenited forms. Where it is not lexically specified, the phonation default is [voiced] under lenition conditions, otherwise it is [voiceless]. For the non-lenited forms [voiceless] is always associated with [oral], so the default statement for these forms must be as in (6.48), which specifies both features on their respective layers.

(6.48) $\begin{bmatrix} \text{PHONATION} \to \text{[voiceless]} \\ \text{VELUM} \to \text{[oral]} \end{bmatrix}$

/m/ needs to be specified as [voiced] and [nasal] in non-lenited forms, which (6.48) does not do. It could be lexically specified as [voiced] except that it occurs as voiceless in assimilated contexts, such as [fɑːsfəɹ] *fàsmhor*, given in section 3.2 above. (If there are speakers who do not assimilate in these circumstances, then /m/ can be lexically specified as [voiced], with a predictive statement to specify [nasal] in non-lenited forms.) This means we need a predictive statement that obligatorily supplies two features, (6.49), so that it will not apply to cases where there are already lexically specified features in those layers.

(6.49)   [lab] → [voiced], [nasal]

This will apply to /m/ but not to /pʰ/ or /p/, both of which have a feature specified lexically on either the phonation or the velic layer.

In the case of the /f/-Ø alternation (6.48) applies to the non-lenited forms, but place and manner cannot have the universal defaults proposed in Lodge (2003a: 941 and refs.), for example. These are [coronal] and [stop], respectively. Without going into a detailed discussion of how to handle alternations with zero here (see, however, Lodge, 1992, 1993, for some suggestions), we need to be able to indicate that in onset position, where we have no specifications at all, this is the appropriate lenited form, but that the defaults of the radical in such cases give us [f]. If we have a situation such as this, we need to be able to represent the potential realization at syllable structure level, as in (6.50).

(6.50)   σ
         ╱ |
            R
            | ╲
           N   C

The onset dependency is indicated, but not labelled. This is intended to represent the fact that the onset may not be realized, but is under certain conditions, in our case the non-lenited form. A statement with the syllable position on the left-hand side of the arrow supplies features as needed, as in (6.51).

(6.51)   ONSET → [labiodental], [fricative]

Under lenition conditions no features are supplied. It is important to make clear that this is not intended to be an illegitimate use of a structure-changing mechanism. The onset dependency in the representation indicates where features can be added; if no features are added, then nothing happens phonetically, there is no structure to be implemented.

We can now see that the three instances of [f] in Gaelic that we saw in section 3.2: radical /f/, lenited /pʰ/ and assimilated, lenited /m/, are clearly separated in the phonology, because they enter into different sorts of relationships with other sounds within the grammar. In (6.52) I give the three sources of [f] with the lexically given features in bold and the redundant features with the statement number that specifies them.

(6.52) /pʰ/	/m/	/f/
[vless]	[vless] (default)	[vless] (6.49)
[oral] (6.47c)	[oral] (6.47c)	[oral] (6.49)
[fric] (6.47a)	[fric] (6.47a)	[fric] (6.51)
[lab]	**[lab]**	[lab] (6.51)

From this we can see that all the lexical representations of [f] are different and biuniqueness does not come into the picture. The phonetic implementation component will interpret the feature arrays in (6.52) accordingly.

In the discussion of lenition I have used the features [labial] and [coronal]. In those languages where [bilabial] and [labiodental] interact phonologically the feature [labial] is needed in the phonological representations. It will be interpreted in the phonetic implementation component appropriately, for example, [labial] + [stop] = involves both lips, in the case under consideration. As regards [coronal], this, too, can be interpreted in the phonetic component as dental or alveolar as appropriate. Where these features contrast, then [dental] and [alveolar] will appear in phonological representations.

6.4.5 'Inserted' vowels in Gaelic

Finally I want to consider the case of vocoid 'insertion', perhaps better *extension* in Scots Gaelic, referred to in section 4.4 and discussed by Hall (2006). Words of this kind are [marəv] *mairbh* 'dead', [kɔɹɔːm] *gorm* 'green', [steɹeːm] *stoirm* 'storm', [faɫaːv] *falbh* 'going', all of which are phonologically monosyllabic. (See also Ladefoged's, 2003: 274–5 discussion of this phenomenon.) There is variation in duration and quality of the 'inserted' vocoid, but such words form an idiosyncratic phonological class. The consonants involved are /l m n r/. In section 4.2 I presented Evans's (1995) representation of a Mayali form with variable realizations: [ɖaʲʔ], [ɖaʲaʔ], [ɖaʔ], 'piece of stringybark', as in (4.4), repeated here as (6.53).

(6.53)   ɹ   ʔ
          \   /
               σ
            /   \
          C   V
          | |
          d   a

Although the features of retroflexion and glottal closure are distributed variably in the speech chain, in each case they are represented
by the same phonological structure. The variation is handled by the
phonetic implementation. So the structure is unordered (cf. Local,
1992, and his quotation from Carnochan, 1957). It would, therefore,
be possible within the approach I am presenting to give a phonological
structure to such words reflecting their monosyllabicity, leaving the
details of implementation to the phonetics. (To that extent the spelling
reflects such a presentation.) *Gorm* can be represented as in (6.54).

(6.54)   σ

                 [round]

                [narrow]
              / |
            O   R
        [oral] | \
      [dorsal] N   C
                 / \
                [lab]

I have used [narrow] as an indicator of coda /r/ (as in my treatment of
German, Lodge, 2003a), though this may have to be amended in the
light of the realizations of actual speakers; the resonance is [back]. I
have also given the representation for /m/ that I used for the onset nasal
above. Even though details of the phonological structure may have to be
altered to account for other aspects of the phonology, the point is that
the phonetic implementation of the nucleus and the first coda consonant
is variable and not to be interpreted necessarily as nucleus *followed by* a
coda. The implementation statements will be of the form of (6.55) with
further phonetic detail depending on which consonant it is.

(6.55)   The contoid articulation (manner and place) of the first coda
         consonant will occur between X% and Y% of the nuclear vocoid
         articulation.

The ordering of the coda consonants as first or second implies that
the nuclear vocoid articulation ceases before the second one, but not,
of course, the roundness and narrowness, which are specified at syllable level.

6.5 CONCLUDING REMARKS

In this chapter I have tried to address the issue of what a declarative, non-segmental, polysystemic phonology might look like. It is
intended to be able to handle the kinds of linguistic phenomena that
have been discussed in the preceding chapters more competently than
the traditional segmental, monosystemic kind, which usually also
admits derivation of one kind or another. By calling the approach
non-segmental, it is not my intention to have no abstract segments
at some levels (onset, coda, foot, word), but to indicate that I do not
assume a priori that speech must be segmented cross-parametrically
at all levels of analysis. Although this approach involves a lot of statements of a local kind, such as those given in the previous sections, it
does not eschew any kind of generalization, where such statements
give insights into the structure of the phonology. And if we are to
take seriously the output of a grammar as actual speech performance,
then, whatever kind of phonological theory we embrace, there will
have to be large amounts of local phonetic implementation. On the
other hand, what are avoided are the many feature changing rules of a
derivational approach and any level equivalent to morphophonemics;
equally there is no need for a systematic phonetic level.

7

PANLECTAL GRAMMARS

ᕕ

It is very doubtful that one can give any clear or useful meaning to the
'everyday sense' of the term 'language' (Chomsky, *Rules and representations*)

7.1 INTRODUCTION

It is generally assumed that we know which language is which and
that consequently we can give a name to each one. But let us take this
question of what English is by considering a few simple answers to see
if they are sufficient. Firstly, we may say that English is the native language of those born in England. This is obviously too narrow because
many speakers in Scotland, Wales, Ireland, Canada, the United States,
Australia, New Zealand and South Africa have English as their native
language. So, we cannot equate a language with a country. English
also has the status of a second language, a lingua franca, in many
countries. This is not primarily to enable the speakers to communi-
cate with native English speakers, but with compatriots who have a
native language other than their own. This situation obtains in parts
of Africa; for instance, in Kenya English is the language of those in
higher education, Kiswahili is the language of Kenyan nationality
and the many ethnic languages are local, tribal markers, for example,
Luo, Kikuyu, Kalenjin. In addition, English serves as an (if not *the*)
international means of communication in many areas of commerce
and travel, for instance. It is the lingua franca of most of the world.
We can see from this that English has long outgrown its parochial
functions of everyday life in the British Isles.

In an attempt to deal with some of the issues I have just mentioned,
writers have tried to define a language with a combination of social
and political factors, and in some cases have added linguistic considerations such as mutual comprehensibility in an attempt to deal
with the problem of variation. (See Romaine, 1982 and Dorian, 1982
on the problems of defining a speech community; see also Fasold,

1984, on nations and languages. Recent studies of this issue, such as Barbour & Carmichael, 2000, place the arguments clearly in the political arena.) If English is associated with a particular country, then it is politics and social considerations that determine the boundaries, not linguistic structures, and mutual comprehensibility does not help in defining a language. Since in the British Isles the dialect continuum does not cover two separate sovereign states, I will look at such an example furnished by what are usually considered varieties of German (see also Boase-Beier & Lodge, 2003). In this case we find that many of the varieties found in Germany are mutually unintelligible, as much as English and Dutch are. The fact that they are closely related languages does not mean that their speakers can each understand one another. Let us take a speaker from the German side of the Dutch–German border and one from Bavaria. If they are speakers of the local dialects, they will understand one another only with the greatest difficulty. In some respects the Plattdeutsch speaker from the north has more in common linguistically speaking with an English speaker, and certainly a speaker of Dutch, than with a Bavarian. For example, the former will have initial [p] and [t] like in English, where the latter has [pf] and [ts], as in *pund* versus *Pfund* and *tien* versus *zehn*, respectively. Despite the fact that they live in the same political entity, Germany, pay the same central taxes, owe allegiance to the same flag, would serve in the Bundeswehr, if they wished to do military service, they do not seem to speak the same language. Furthermore, northern speakers will be able to understand their Dutch neighbours far better than they can understand their Bavarian compatriots. There is an important sense in which the north German and the Dutch speakers speak the same language. From a linguistic point of view their national allegiance is irrelevant. Of course, they are each taught a different standard language in school, but this, too, is a political and social matter not a linguistic one. The picture we end up with, if we look at geographical variation in language, is of a dialect continuum, a slowly changing set of partially overlapping linguistic systems, which at the extremities may be very different indeed.

From a linguistic point of view it would be convenient if linguists could define a language by its structural characteristics. This is implicit in the notion of a panlectal grammar (Bailey, 1973): one language has one grammar, so New York English, Birmingham English and East African English are varieties of the *same* language. This is high-level linguistic sameness. Any variation in form is considered to be relatively superficial and can be accounted for by differences in the rule system relating the stored lexical forms of the native speakers to their realizations in phonetic substance. For instance, English rhotic and non-rhotic accents can be seen as minor variations in the substance. A panlectal approach will propose a single underlying, phonological form for each such word and the phonetic forms will be derived from it by different rules. In this case the rhotic forms are taken as underlying and a rule deleting /r/ after tautosyllabic vowels will account for the non-rhotic versions. This kind of approach is often implicit in discussions of varieties, as in the example of Carr's exercise on English /r/ in his coursebook on phonology (1993a: 41–2, answer: 307). Basically, this relies on two (ordered) rules, as in (7.1) and (7.2).

(7.1)   /r/-deletion
         /r/ → Ø / V ___ (C)$

(7.2)   /r/-realization
         /r/ → [ɹ]

In (7.3) we can see how the operation of the extra rule of /r/-deletion produces the difference between rhotic and non-rhotic accents. So rhotic speakers and non-rhotic speakers order their rules differently. (It is not always clear whether both types of speaker are assumed to have both rules; rhotic speakers either order (7.2) first, so that (7.1) applies vacuously, or do not have (7.1) in their grammar.)

(7.3)   /kar/   /farm/   /kar/   /farm/
     /r/-deletion   --   --   [kɑ]   [fam]   (non-rhotic)
     /r/-realization [kɑɹ] [fɑɹm]   --   --   (rhotic)

Lowland Scots and RP are thus related to one another by a rule of coda /r/-deletion. This assumes that speakers of RP know where Lowland Scots speakers have lexical coda /r/. There is, however, plenty of evidence to show that this is not the case; in fact, non-rhotic English speakers generally cannot predict rhotic forms accurately. Trudgill (1983: 8–30) shows how relatively poor native speakers of English are at recognizing forms of their own language that they do not themselves use, and, in a separate paper, looks at a number of linguistic features of British pop singers in the 1960s and 1970s, among them rhoticity (1983: 141–60). Hypercorrect forms such as [əɹ bætʃələɹ bɔɹ] *a bachelor boy* and [sɔːɹ ðɛm] *saw them* are frequent (see 1983: 149) in the singers' attempts to sound American. If the grammar represents a native speaker's knowledge, which enables him or her to predict all forms of his or her system and produce them when needed, then how are we to explain these anomalous forms? They occur too often to be explained away as slips of the tongue. Rather they are mistaken analyses of a target variety on the basis of the speaker's own system. The rule that non-rhotic speakers invent is something like the following: 'Insert [ɹ] after the vowels [ɑ ɜ ɔ ə].'

Of course, such a dichotomous presentation of accents as rhotic or non-rhotic overlooks the fact that there is often a cline from some obstruent realization (for example, a trill or tap) through a range of possible articulations to no apparent phonetic presence. For instance, one of the informants from Edinburgh for Lodge (1984: 82–5) has the following forms: [əwɛr] *aware*, [ʌɛðər̩] *whether*, [püəɹ] *poor*, [koət] *court*, [bʌdz̥] *birds*, [pɔʃʌ] *posher* and [fʌːst] *first*, with varying 'degrees of rhoticity'. So, phonetic implementation of the lexical forms is going to be less straightforward than presented in (7.1) and (7.2). Similarly, in Lancashire, where some urban areas have rhoticity, there is variation between speakers as to whether they have a coda retroflex approximant, or a general retroflex posture (Honikman's, 1964 articulatory setting), for example, in [bɜɻ̩n̩l̩ë] or [bɜn̩l̩ë] *Burnley*. (Note that the latter has no 'compensatory lengthening' of the vowel phase.)

Chomsky (1980: 117–20) concludes that the notion of a language (that is, 'English', 'French', 'German') is of little use to linguists, who should concentrate on grammars. If we follow this line of reasoning, it means that we end up with a set of grammars some of which overlap fairly closely, others of which do not, but all need to be described separately. It could be suggested that comprehension will take place in those cases where overlap is greatest. A large part of this overlap will be in the lexical forms of the varieties in question, but, to my knowledge, no one has tried to correlate the amount of overlap with the degree of comprehension, though Trudgill (1983: 29–30) makes some tentative suggestions in this regard. However, comprehensibility is not necessarily commensurate with linguistic overlap. For example, most broad speakers from the north of England have no difficulty in understanding RP-speaking newsreaders on the radio and television, but the systems do not overlap very much at the phonological level, especially as regards phonetic implementation. And the RP speaker may have more difficulty understanding a northerner than the other way round. This has to do with currency and exposure to some extent: RP is heard fairly frequently in the media, broad northern varieties less so, though since roughly the mid-1990s fewer RP speakers are heard on British television. However, the extent to which accents in the media affect individual speakers is far from clear. Whereas a Bolton (Lancashire) accent may be heard in popular programmes from time to time (for example, the comedian Peter Kay or the late demolition and steam traction expert Fred Dibnah), we do not find newsreaders who are obviously from Bolton, or from Norfolk, or from Birmingham, even though there are plenty of 'regional' varieties to be heard in news broadcasts, in particular Scottish, Irish and Welsh. In other words, which accents are heard in the media and the programmes in which they are heard are controlled and socially determined, and it is largely a matter of fashion. The formerly ubiquitous RP accent of television and radio announcers has given way not to the locally determined, indigenous varieties, but to a carefully selected set of regional accents. In the 1960s, in the wake of The Beatles, the Liverpudlian accent was the hallmark of the age, but it has disappeared from the media scene, and its populist position has been filled by the supposedly anti-establishment, so-called Estuary English. But the key to linguistic variation and change is more likely to be everyday face-to-face interaction, not experience via the media, which might encourage copying as opposed to interaction. (For a discussion of this issue, see Trudgill, 1986: 40–1.)

The implication of the panlectal approach to the phonology of a language is that all speakers of English have knowledge as native speakers as to where coda /r/ can occur in all varieties, which would mean that they could be rhotic or non-rhotic at will. Trudgill (1983, as presented above) has demonstrated clearly that native speakers cannot recognize, let alone predict and produce correctly, all varieties of English. One further point needs noting in respect of rhoticity, however. There are clear signs that in the United States and in Britain many speakers produce 'hyperrhotic' forms such as [θɔɹt] *thought* (see, for instance, Trudgill, 1986: 71–8, for a discussion, and a recent paper by Krämer, 2008). Of course, the explanation for this spread could well be that since rhotic forms are prestigious in America at least, hypercorrect forms take hold more easily than in England, where the prestige accent is non-rhotic. In other cases hyperrhoticity can be seen as an indication of dialect loss, that is, speakers no longer know the details of their traditional local accent or dialect. Whether the hyperrhotic accents become established as models for acquisition remains to be seen. But the evidence against panlectal grammars does not rest solely on rhoticity. That it is not just a matter of rhoticity can be seen in other cases of hypercorrection which are a matter of phonological contrast as opposed to the phonotactic distinction involved in rhoticity. In Lodge (1984: 15) I refer to those speakers in the north of England who try to copy RP speech with its /ʊ/ – /ʌ/ distinction as in *put, butcher* and *putt, come*, respectively. Most of them produce a vocoid articulation of the following kind: [ə]˞ [æ̈], but they use it in both lexical sets, that is, in *put, butcher, putt* and *come*. What they are actually doing is using their own underlying phonological system, which has no distinction, but changing the phonetic realization to sound more like the target realization of RP /ʌ/.

Even polylectal grammars, which cover a restricted number of varieties, cannot be defined other than by linguistic criteria. That is to say, one single grammar may account for a number of different realizations with just minor rule variation, often at the level of realization, but they do not coincide with social groupings. Trudgill (1974) attempts to describe all the varieties of Norwich with one system (diasystem), but this ignores the fact that, say, most young speakers from the city do not know the distinction between /ɛː/ as in *gate* and /æɪ/ as in *gait*, used only by the very oldest inhabitants and rural speakers in Norfolk (see Trudgill, 1974, and Lodge, 2001). That they may recognize individual forms as 'the way grandad speaks', for instance, is no more knowledge of the system than knowing that *chat* is French for 'cat' and *chien* French for 'dog' indicates an ability to speak French.

The picture I presented above of a Dutch–German dialect continuum is handled by positing a set of overlapping linguistic systems, which at each end may be very different, as different as standard Dutch and standard German. The same applies to linguistic varieties of English on mainland Britain. Dialects merge into one another, changes occur subtly over a few miles. It is only convenience that leads us to label them 'Norfolk dialect', 'a Yorkshire accent', 'Scouse'. Such labels are no more accurate from a linguistic point of view than the language labels I discussed above. 'Norfolk dialect' belongs to the group with an /ʊ/ – /ʌ/ distinction, but then what of those speakers in the far west of the county, in the Fens bordering Cambridgeshire and Lincolnshire, who vary between [ʊ] and [ʌ] in many words, or those who have only [ʊ]? Aren't they 'real' Norfolk speakers? (Recall our discussion of the defining characteristics of the standard English king of hearts in Chapter 1.) The fact of the matter is that there are no clear-cut linguistic boundaries that stop at the county line; the systems merge and interact in interesting ways, and variation, even in one and the same speaker, is the order of the day. Most speakers (except for those who lead very isolated lives) have a number of overlapping systems at their disposal, which they use on different social occasions. Needless to say, British English and American English do not form a dialect continuum in the way varieties on mainland Britain do. Time and space have brought about changes in each which were unconnected. Of course, with the increase in worldwide communication these geographical obstacles become less and less significant. A thousand years ago the Fens were, indeed, an area that was difficult to travel through and so constituted a real barrier. Today, however, they are not significant in these terms. Distance, too, is less important today with our road, rail and air transport. Communications between, say, Manchester and Liverpool are easy and that has an effect on linguistic interaction. In some cases connections between major cities may be more effective than between a city and its surrounding area, for example, between Manchester and nearby Pennine villages. But this does not mean that panlectal or polylectal grammars are justifiable. I shall return below to a consideration of polylectal grammars and the way in which the abstraction of phonological forms may be applicable to this particular issue.

7.2 LEVELS OF VARIATION

Let us consider now the kinds of phonological variation that take place. The following types of variation relate to different aspects of phonology, as discussed by Petyt (1980), all exemplified from English:

1. contrastive differences: *could* and *cud* have contrasting vowels or are homophonous. This involves a different number of vowel contrasts in the two types of accent;
2. 'allophonic' differences: [ʔ] may be a realizational variant of /t/ or of /p t k/. Many accents of English have the glottal stop as a realization of /t/ only, but others, such as London varieties and some Norfolk ones, have it as a contextually determined realization of any of the so-called voiceless stops, for example, Cockney [kʰaʔ ə tsɔɪ] *cup of tea*, [leʔɐ] *letter*, [ɑ laɪʔ jɐ] *I like you*; Norfolk [pʰɹiʔɬ] *people*, [sɹi jəʔmɑːɹə] *see you tomorrow*, [lʌɪʔ jɐː] *like you*;
3. realizational differences: /æ/ ('short a') may be realized as [æ] (RP), [a] (Manchester), or [ɑ] (Belfast);
4. phonotactic differences: coda /r/ is permitted (rhotic accents) or is not permitted (non-rhotic);

5. lexical incidence differences: *path*, *class* and *dance* have the same vowel as *start* or as *man* depending on the accent.

Hypercorrection is important evidence for lack of systemic overlap. It is important to note that there are two different phenomena referred to as hypercorrection: Labov (1966) uses it to refer to the 'cross-over effect' of a group of speakers using a variable form more than the group of speakers they aspire to copy, as in the case of coda /r/ in New York; alternatively, it can be used to refer to the use of forms that belong to no one's native phonological system, as in the use of pronunciations such as [ɑfɹɪkə] *Africa*, based on an incorrect extension of the backing and lengthening of /æ/ in many southern accents of British English and RP from forms such as *after*, *craft*, *laugh*. Both types are the over-application of a phonological feature, but in the first type it is within the bounds of the grammatical system. The second type is more significant from a phonological point of view in that it reflects a lack of knowledge of the target system in the same way as L2-learners extend their L1 system to cover areas of the grammar of L2 of which they are unsure. It could be argued that learning someone else's accent is very similar to learning someone else's language, the difference being that most of the lexis and syntax will be the same in the first case, but not in the second. This is part of the degrees of overlap between systems.

In the next two sections I want to consider interpretations of sameness or difference at phonological (section 7.3) and lexical levels (section 7.4). The lexical examples involve (mis)interpretation of the realizations.

7.3 MERGERS

Since we are dealing with language change when we consider the sociolinguistic effects of variation, one of the issues related to systemic change is that of mergers of phonological distinctions. We ask, have these two formerly distinct phonological units merged into one? In other words, are they the same unit now? (Note that the northern English accents with no /ʊ/ – /ʌ/ distinction have not undergone a merger; from a historical perspective Middle English /ʊ/ split into two in the more southerly dialects.)

The first example I should like to discuss is the phenomenon of /f/–/θ/ variation in British English accents. In some accents /f/ and /θ/ may genuinely have fallen together as /f/, but in others there is evidence that this is not the case. So, (7.4) would represent realizations of a merged /f/, but compare these realizations with those in (7.5), potential evidence of non-merger.

(7.4)   [pæʔ fɪŋks]   Pat thinks
         [lɪz fɪŋks]   Liz thinks

(7.5)   [pæʔ fɪŋks]   Pat thinks
         [lɪz sɪŋks]   Liz thinks

In the last example the sibilant assimilation found in speakers who use [θ] occurs in the same environment in the speakers under consideration. On the other hand, such a speaker would not assimilate any /f/ in these circumstances any more than speakers who use the forms in (7.4) or those with the /f/ – /θ/ distinction would do, as, for example, in (7.6).

(7.6)   [pæʔ faɪnz]   Pat finds
         [lɪz faɪnz]   Liz finds
        *[lɪz saɪnz]   Liz finds

Clearly, though, it would be odd for any analyst to say that for such speakers /θ/ has two allophones [f] and [s] (but no [θ]), if fully specified phonemes were assumed. On the other hand, an underspecified phonological representation, even a segmental one, could manage to cover the three different types of speaker: (1) those with alternating [f~s], which I will symbolize /F/, and /f/, (2) those with just /f/ and (3) those with /f/ and /θ/. My suggestion in Lodge (1992: 29) is that /θ/ is represented as [voiceless] and [dental] underlyingly, but this cannot work for speakers who assimilate onset /θ/ to a preceding coda /s/, since place of articulation changes. Whereas speakers of type (3) could have the place feature [coronal] specified, interpreted differently by phonetic implementation according to the environment (see section 6.4.4 above on the phonetic implementation of [coronal]), this cannot be the case for type (1) speakers, since they have labiodental realizations. It would be possible to alter the lexically specified features for /F/ for such speakers to just [oral]. There would have to be a predictive statement to the effect that lexical [oral] implied [voiceless] and [fricative], as in (7.7).

(7.7)   [oral] → [voiceless], [fricative]

The place feature would either be [alveolar] attached at ambisyllabic coda/onset level in the assimilating cases (see section 6.2 above), and

[oral] would predict [labiodental] in the other cases. No phonological distinction needs to be made between /f/ and /θ/ for speakers of type (2). So the three grammars differ slightly from one another: type (2) has only /f/ in the phonological representations; type (3) has /θ/ specified as [coronal] and type (1) has a distinctive unit /F/, represented as just [oral].

I now want to consider some vowel distinctions from English, which are variable in East Anglia. Trudgill & Foxcroft (1978) discuss the *beer/bear* distinction and its merger in various parts of East Anglia. The realizations for a large number of speakers in both lexical sets are in the region of [ɛː], and is considered to be a merger. This is reflected even in local dialect poetry and other written representations of dialect forms. Trudgill & Foxcroft (1978: 75–7) wanted to see if there were generational differences in the maintenance of this merger and whether London speech, which has the distinction and was spreading from the south-west, was having any effect. For whatever reasons, it became apparent that for some young speakers the two lexical sets have passed through each other's phonetic space, as it were, so that the vowel of the *beer*-set was realized in the vicinity of [ɛː] and the vowel of the *bare*-set was [eː] with a closer articulation. Whether it is appropriate to talk about merger and de-merger in cases like this is not at all clear, but we can see that the notion of phonological sameness has to be treated very carefully. In the case of East Anglia we have some speakers with the distinction and some without. Those who have no distinction often produce hypercorrect forms, especially when interacting with non-East Anglian speakers, such as [tɪə] instead of [tɛː] in *tear (up the paper)*. This is clearly a case of accents in contact and interacting; a discussion of this complex phenomenon goes beyond the scope of the present book, but see Trudgill (1986) for the discussion of a number of examples.

The other East Anglian vowel distinction I want to consider is by now restricted to rural Norfolk speakers, but in phonetic terms it can be considered in relation to the vocoid articulations discussed in the previous paragraph. The Middle English distinction between *made* and *maid* is still maintained by some, mostly older speakers with the realizations [mɛːd] and [mæɪd], respectively. If we use phonetic similarity as a criterion of phonological sameness, then why not consider *made* as belonging to the same lexical set as *beer/bare*? Since these vowels come from very different historical origins, ME /aː/ and ME /Vr/, respectively, analysts are not tempted to suggest such a solution (for example, it is not part of Trudgill's, 1974 proposals). The different historical origins have resulted in different distributions and behaviour. Words of the *make*-set always end in a consonant and so to that extent belong to the so-called short vowels – that is, those that can only occur in closed syllables, irrespective of their actual duration (see section 5.7 above, and the examples in (5.10)). On the other hand, words with historical coda /r/ have linking [ɹ] before another vowel. Of course, it could be argued that since vowels in the *make*-set and the /Vr/-vowels are in complementary distribution, there is still no evidence that they have not merged. However, there is sociolinguistic evidence that is important and relevant to our discussion. Speakers who have the *made/maid* distinction are aware that it is a local, 'in-group' linguistic feature. Outsiders, whether from Norfolk or further afield, do not have this distinction, so the former group change their linguistic behaviour and use [æɪ] in the *make*-set, merging *made* and *maid*, as most other English speakers have done. This sociolinguistic sensitivity does not occur with words of the *beer/bare*-set, and no hypercorrection occurs either, which indicates a clear separation of the two lexical sets, despite the overlap of the [ɛː] realizations.

One issue that is thrown up by the merger of *made* and *maid* in Norfolk is how mergers come about. We may be aware of realizations of phonological units spread around a particular focus of phonetic space. This is easy to imagine with vocoid articulations, since there is no contact between the tongue surface and the upper part of the mouth, but it applies equally to places and manners of contact. Such realizations can move gradually from one location to another. (For a discussion in some detail of the effects of this on phonological categories, see Silverman, 2006, especially Chapters 5 and 6.) Gradual movement through phonetic space is what Trudgill & Foxcroft (1978) study in relation to the realizations of particular vowel distinctions. On the other hand, it is equally possible for systemic change to come about through contact between the speakers of two different systems, so that some speakers take on the forms of a system not originally their own. This could account for the young East Anglian speakers taking on the London-based distinction of the *beer* and *bare* sets, or the replacement of traditional Norfolk [ɛː] in *made* by another regional, but non-distinctive variant realization [æɪ]. Replacement is a more abrupt development than merger. The latter is system-internal, the former is the result of the interaction of different varieties.

Some mergers, apparently purely phonetic in nature, are accepted as such in historical terms, but there are plenty of other instances, such as those discussed above, that need clear functional criteria to determine whether a merger has taken place. Examples of mergers from the history of English include the following:

/e:/ versus /ɛ:/ in *meet/meat*
/a:/ versus /ai/ in *name/day*
/x/-loss leading to mergers in *might/mite*

though, as we have already seen in one case, there is dialect variation in respect of all of these; for example, the retention of the *meet/meat* distinction in parts of the Lake District, and the loss of /x/ later in the northern dialects leading to the maintenance of distinctions such as *port* with [ɔ:] and *thought* with [ɔu] (see, for example, Lodge, 1973).

What I want to consider now are a few examples of lexical sameness from different dialects of English. The lexical interpretation of some variant forms of English relies on the imposition of a panlectal set of lexical items based on the written standard.

7.4 LEXICAL MERGERS AND STANDARDIZATION

Sameness of linguistic form is sometimes assumed in cases where historical processes have obscured the origins of the assumed variants. Four examples from English will suffice to show slightly different ways in which false identifications can occur. Firstly, the modern English present participial suffixes -*ing* and -*in'* are typically related to one another via 'g-dropping' (for example, Chomsky & Halle, 1968: 85, and Labov, 1972: 240). This is clearly a shorthand, based on orthographic convention: *ing* versus *in'*, for a complicated historical development. Lass (1992: 144–6) and Fischer (1992: 250–6) present details of the way in which two separate suffixes became confused and reinterpreted. The phonological and phonetic aspects of this 'merger' are of particular interest. The Old English participial suffix was -*end(e)*, which lost its final [d] during the early Middle English period. A variable vocoid quality is quite likely, given the modern accent variation for the suffix. The deverbal noun suffix was -*ung*; this form was used in a number of constructions, including the analytical progressive of the verb, formed with *to be* + *on* + gerund. The vowel of the suffix changed its quality to [ɪ] and the preposition became a schwa; cf. dialectal and archaic standard *he's a-coming*. So, originally, the -*ing* suffix was nominal. Given their use in two different forms of the progressive and the phonological changes they were subject to, in particular vowel reduction, the scene was set for the confusion and conflation of the two suffixes [ɪn] and [ɪŋg]. The distinction between the verbal and nominal uses, respectively, was gradually lost (see, however, claims that it has not been lost in all English dialects in Houston, 1985). By the late Middle English period [ɪn], orthographically *in/yn*, can be found for the gerund alongside the *-ing* form, for example, in the Paston letters, as in (7.8), from Warrington (1956: 255), from a letter by Agnes Paston to her husband William written before 1440.

(7.8)   I sende yow gode tydyngges of þe comyng and brynggyn hoom of
         þe Gentylwomman

So, rather than actually merging, the two suffixes were used as alternatives for a while. As the standardized written form of the language developed, the *-ing* form was chosen as the 'proper' form. In speech, on the other hand, *-in'* continued to be used. In modern dialects (with the exception of those discussed by Houston, 1985) speakers either use [ɪn] exclusively or [ɪn] and [ɪŋ] variably. At some stage, probably during the nineteenth century, the spelling *-in'* was adopted as the standard way of representing the non-standard form.

What the label g-dropping fails to acknowledge is that this alternation is functional not phonological in origin. Indeed, it is difficult to see how [ɪŋg] could possibly become [ɪn] in unstressed syllables by the removal of the stop articulation. The loss of the final stop leaves a homorganic nasal, hence modern English [ɪŋ]. This is the problem with the SPE analysis of [ŋ] as /ng/, so that removal of the /g/ leaves /n/ = [n], as a description of the historical process. (Of course, if one assumes that both /n/ and /ŋ/ are phonemes, then 'g-dropping' can only refer to the spelling.) The point is that, whereas an abstract analysis of [ŋ] as /ng/ in all cases allows us to claim that the [-ɪn] forms are accounted for by ordering /g/-deletion before assimilation, this makes no sense as a description of the historical process, since historical change operates in its initial stages on phonetic forms, not on abstract phonological ones. In other words, the pronunciation of /-ng/ was always [-ŋg], so loss of the final stop gives us the standard and southern forms in [-ŋ]. This appears to be yet another instance of the confusion of levels.

We might be tempted to say that there is phonological – as opposed to morphological – evidence that the *-in'* is related to stress, since we find it in other words that are not participles or gerunds in unstressed syllables: *somethin', anythin', nothin', mornin', evenin'*. This would then be a historical development of Middle English [-ɪŋg] in all such cases. Of course, it should be pointed out that during the Middle

English period final voiced stops after nasals were unstable, and both /b/ and /ɡ/ disappeared in this position (the latter not in parts of the north of England) and /d/ did in the case of *-end*. In some accents today /d/ still exhibits this instability, especially before another consonant (see Lodge, 1984). However, in each case the resultant nasal is homorganic with the lost stop, for example, [læm] *lamb* and [kɪŋ] *king*. But, as I have just pointed out, the resultant [-n]-form is difficult to account for as a loss of [ɡ] in the non-participial unstressed *-(th)ing* forms, unless they are analogical forms based on the participial form. But, finally, there is no reason why participial *-in'* and *-thin'* endings should be treated as the same; a polysystemic approach treats them differently, as they are from different parts of the grammar (whether analogy is involved or not).

The next example is very similar: *them/'em*. The former is a Scandinavian borrowing along with *they*, and the latter is the Middle English reflex of the Old English *hem*. Indeed, in Chaucer's writings *they* is the subject form and *hem* the object form. Once again, the standardization process makes *them* the correct form and *'em* is seen as the spoken version of it, though the /ð/-deletion rule is word-specific; for instance, there is no equivalent *[daʊnt eɪ] *don't they?* etc. On the basis of examples like these, *-ing* and *them*, it would be possible to argue that there are two grammars in this respect, one based on speaking, one on writing, and that when speaking some people switch between the two. There will also be speakers who do not use the standard written forms in speech. So, rather than trying to produce a single grammar of English to account for this sort of variation, I am proposing that speakers grammar-switch under various circumstances. Code-switching is well attested in bilinguals, so why not in monolinguals at this grammatical level? In fact, we might want to describe all such switching, whether bilingual, multilingual or monolingual, as grammar-switching. In cases such as these from English there is no need to have recourse to the notion of merger.

The two final examples are simply instances of lexical misinterpretation with no suggestion of a merger. The first is once again from Norfolk dialect. In this, unlike in most dialects of English, there is a form, [ət/əʔ], used as the unstressed object form in cases such as (7.9)–(7.12), where I have used the standard orthographic representation *it*.

(7.9)   [ɡɪv əʔ]   give it
(7.10) [hɪt əʔ]   hit it

(7.11) [ɪz ə?] is it?
(7.12) [ɛnt ə?] ain't it?

It also triggers smoothing (cf. section 5.7 above), as in (7.13), where the monophthongal realization indicates lexical /uː/ followed by /ə/.

(7.13) [dɜː?] do it.

All such cases are interpreted as *it* (cf. Trudgill, 1974).

On the other hand, the subject form is *that*, as in *That's raining, that is, that's right,* and no form of *it* is used in these cases. The realizations of *that* vary somewhat, depending on stress, for example, [ðæ?/ðɑ?/ɑ?/ɐ?], and *that's* may be [as]/[ɐs] (cf. Trudgill, 1974), as in (7.14).

(7.14) [ɐ(?)s ɛvə sə nʌɪs] That's ever so nice.

It is only the standard written form that makes us identify [ət/ə?] as *it*, as in the preceding orthographic representations; there is no reason not to interpret it as the object form of *that*, which can lose its initial consonant even in subject position. In this case we are not dealing with grammar-switching as much as a misinterpretation of the object form of the pronoun via the standard language (and most other English dialects).

The final example is a dialectal form that is difficult to interpret: the definite article in many northern English varieties. Typically it is realized as [?] (cf. Wells, 1982; Lodge, 1984), as in (7.15)–(7.17).

(7.15) [ɪŋ?gaːdn] in the garden
(7.16) [gɪvəs?bɹuum] Give us the broom.
(7.17) [avjəgɑ??taɛm] Have you got the time?

Note that (7.17) is different from (7.18) in that the glottal closure is longer in the former.

(7.18) [avjəgɑ?taɛm] Have you got time?

It also occurs utterance-initially as a closed glottis onset to a voiced stop, as in (7.19).

(7.19) [?busɪzkʊmɪn] The bus is coming.

In Middle English there were two forms of the definite article, one with initial [t], one with [θ], the former written with *t*, the other with *th* (or a thorn, þ, as in (7.8) above). The former is interpreted as an assimilated form. (The latter was later voiced in unstressed position like other [θ]-initial words.) In standard English the reflexes of the *te* form have disappeared through phonological simplifications, for example, *at te last > atte last > at last*. In the north, however, the glottal stop form is presumably the descendant of the [t]-initial form, though the development is not necessarily straightforward, as pointed out in Jones (2002). An interesting development found to the west of the Pennines, mostly in Lancashire, is the complementary distribution of the [ʔ] and [θ] variants such that the pattern is: [ʔ] + consonant, as in the examples above, and [θ] + vowel, as in (7.20) and (7.21).

(7.20) [θɛːɹɪəɫ]   the aerial
(7.21) [θɑspɪɫ]   the hospital

And there may even be both realizations together in some contexts:

(7.22) [wɪʔθɛːɹɪəɫ]   with the aerial
(7.23) [ɪnʔθɑspɪɫ]   in the hospital

For some older speakers the distribution can even be [ʔ] + consonant, [t] + vowel.

In addition to this dialectal form, many speakers use standard English [ðɪ]/[ðə] forms. For example, in Lodge (1984: 36) speaker N makes the following utterances in close succession:

(7.24) [dæʊnʔsɛllə]   down the cellar
        [teːksθɛːɹeəɫ]   takes the aerial
        [wɛːjəgɛʔðeɛːɹeəɫ]   where you get the aerial

(The lengthened lateral in *cellar* is not a normal part of his phonology.) Here again we can talk of grammar-switching between local and standard grammars. Rupp & Page-Verhoeff (2005) claim that there is a semantic/pragmatic difference between the use of *the* and what is often referred to as Definite Article Reduction (DAR) – that is, the forms being discussed in this section. The categories they propose are hard to apply in the examples recorded for Lodge (1984), but if all speakers who use both *the* and DAR do make such distinctions, then both forms are part of the same grammar. I have little data on this point to decide one way or the other. Further investigations are needed. (For a much more detailed phonetic investigation of the phenomenon, see Jones, 2007.)

7.5 ABSTRACTNESS AND POLYLECTAL GRAMMARS

An aspect of abstractness in phonology that was not discussed in Chapter 5, but can be considered here, is its relevance to panlectal grammars. This is a matter of high-level sameness or difference. Even though notions such as 'the English language', 'the French language' underlie a lot of published work in linguistics, we have set them aside as unhelpful linguistic concepts. On the other hand, we can investigate the possibilities presented by abstraction of having lexical entry forms that cover several linguistic varieties. This is certainly implicit in Fudge (1969) in which he uses totally abstract phonological elements to describe English syllable structure. For instance, he says (1969: 269–70):

> The inclusion of post-vocalic r (places 4 and 5 [in the syllable; KRL]) must not be taken as implying that the scheme does not apply to 'r-less' dialects: D3 is an abstract element which in some dialects (notably RP) may often have no realization of its own, but which will, so to speak, contribute to the realization of the preceding vowel.

This suggests that abstraction, with little or no phonetic content in phonological structures, makes panlectal, or, at least, polylectal grammars easier to devise, though such an approach ignores the problem of native-speaker knowledge discussed above. The question will be whether differences of realization are to be accounted for at the lexical level or elsewhere, and what that 'elsewhere' might be. It certainly seems attractive to be able to account for all vocalic variation in English in such abstract terms, giving a lot more work for the phonetic implementation component. In Fudge's proposal even vowel + coda /r/ realizations will be handled in this way. So, using IPA symbols rather than Fudge's original formulae, /ɛr/, as in *serve*, for instance, would be implemented as [ɛɹ] in some rhotic accents, [ɝ] in others and [ɜː] in non-rhotic ones. But the question still remains, how far can one go in connecting different accents of a language? Eventually there will be phonological representations for vowels that very few people recognize, for example, /ɛː/ from Middle English /aː/ in *make* that we discussed in section 7.3 above, or reflexes of Middle English /x/ making vowel distinctions between *port* and *thought*, *wait* and *weight* in many northern varieties, also referred to above. Such differences will have consequences for storage forms of the same lexical item in different accents. So extreme abstractness of the kind proposed by Fudge does not solve the 'one language' issue any more than the derivational approach of SPE with its abstract phonological forms (including /x/).

As we have already pointed out, if we want to capture native speaker knowledge with our grammars, then a grammar can only account for a limited number of varieties. This does not mean that polylectal grammars work better in the sense in which they are normally applied. That is, a polylectal account takes a geographically or socially prescribed area, the home of a 'speech community', as its focus – for example, Norwich, as described by Trudgill (1974). But since this also cuts across native speaker knowledge in that very often different generations have (slightly) different systems (compare the informants in Stockport, for example, in Lodge, 1984), we need to describe the linguistic overlap of the relevant systems as well as the differences.

Of the types of phonological variation given above in section 7.2 only some can be handled by means of underspecification and systemic overlap. Type (1), contrastive differences, (for example, *could* versus *cud*) and type (4), phonotactic differences, (for example, rhotic/non-rhotic) furnish evidence of different systems, whereas type (3), realizational differences, can be treated under sameness of underlying unit. For example, /æ/, realized as [æ] (RP), [a] (Manchester) or [ɑ] (Belfast) can be treated as the same vowel by specifying it as [low] in lexical entries; phonetic implementation will interpret it as [front], [central] or [back] accordingly. Type (2), 'allophonic' differences, are not handled in the same way in a polysystemic approach, as we saw in Chapter 6, so coda [ʔ] may or may not be associated with onset /t/ or /p t k/ depending on the rest of the system. The example I gave in Chapter 2 (see example (2.2)) would suggest that there are two accent types: those that have alternating glottal stop and oral stop(s), and those that do not. Systemic overlap is not appropriate in this case. Similarly, type (5), lexical incidence differences, since they are distributional, may involve different systems. Whereas *economics* with initial /ɪi/ or /e/, or *scone* with /oʊ/ or /ɒ/, are minimally different and individually determined, speakers with /a/ in *path, grass, France* etc. cannot predict properly the distribution in those accents which have /ɑ/ in such words. This is not a matter of meaningful contrast, because accents with /a/ in such words also have an /ɑ/-type vowel (usually realized as [ɑː]), as in *park, calm.*

As an example of how system overlap can be treated in abstract terms, irrespective of geographical origin, I will take English three-consonant onsets. The basic pattern is as in (7.25).

(7.25)   /s/ + voiceless stop + approximant

The category approximant covers /j w r l/; note that the approximant in [juu] is classified here as a consonant. The syllable structure of such onsets is as in (7.26). Since C_2C_3 mimic the phonotactic constraints of two-consonant onsets, the /s/ is interpreted as dependent on their structure.

(7.26)   O

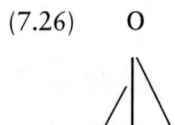

I will concentrate on those clusters that involve one of the first three consonants, not /l/. If we take their phonological representations in single consonant onsets to be as in (7.27) (from Lodge, 1992: 29), then we can see whether they apply in three-consonant ones as well.

(7.27)   j   w   r
                    [round]
            [front]   [central]

In the case of [-w]-onsets the attachment of [round] must be at the highest onset level (or higher, if the nuclear vocoid articulation is also round), as in (7.28).

(7.28)   O

          [round]

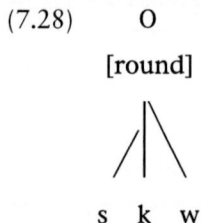

          s   k   w

(The other two possibilities /spw/ and /stw/ do not occur; the former is ruled out by a constraint on [bilabial] over two consonant places and the latter simply is not found in any words, although /tw-/ is legitimate as a two-consonant onset.)

   At onset level, [front] and [central] are also attached, as in (7.29), in which I give all the possible distinctive onsets with /j/ and /r/.

(7.29)   O   O

          [front]   [central]

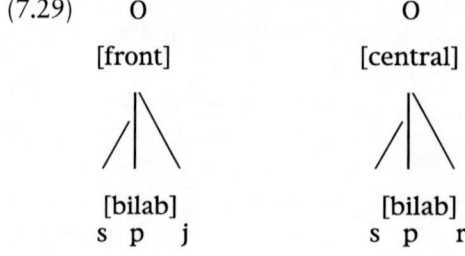

          [bilab]   [bilab]
          s   p   j   s   p   r

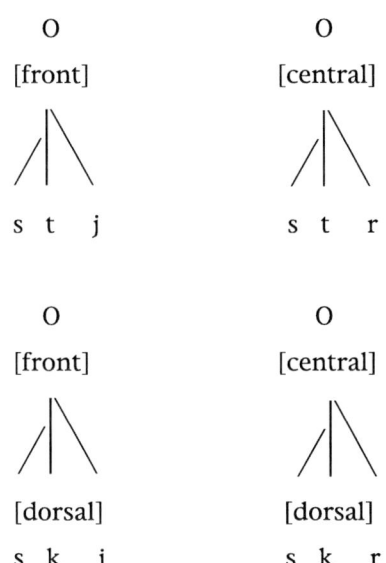

These structures are sufficiently distinct from one another and any other onset types to make them capable of interpretation by the phonetic implementation component. In earlier discussions in Chapter 6 predictable features were supplied for all layers for the phonetic implementation to interpret, but in the case of English three-consonant onsets there is no need to do this because of the restricted number of features that can apply. So any structure of the kind in (7.29) will be interpreted as starting with a voiceless oral fricative with the appropriate lip position and resonance. This will change to a stop articulation at the specified place, or as alveolar by default, moving to the approximation at the end of the onset. The only predictive statements we need to make relate to the place of the approximation, as in (7.30) and (7.31).

(7.30) [front] → [dorsal]
(7.31) [round] → [back], [dorsal]

Voicing starts at some point during the approximation, so a statement similar to the one given in (6.27) above is needed.

Variation in the realization of three-consonant onsets occurs in particular in terms of place of the approximation and place of the friction and closure. The whole of the articulation of the onset is affected by the kind of approximation used. The different kinds of phonetic implementation can be applied to the structures in (7.29), so palato-alveolar, alveolo-palatal and post-alveolar points of contact are all referred back to a single underlying structure. In (7.32) I give a selection of possible realizations.

(7.32)   [ʃtɹ-]   [ʃtj-]   [ʃtʃ-]   [ʃkɹ-]   [ʃkj-]

These are only some of the possibilities, and they are fairly broadly transcribed, but the point I am making here is that as far as three-consonant onsets in English are concerned a single phonological structure can cover a whole range of realizations.

Any exceptions to the constraints on onsets, such as /smj-/ in *smew* and /sfr-/ in *sphragistics* will have the unusual features specified in their lexical forms, as in (7.33).

(7.33)

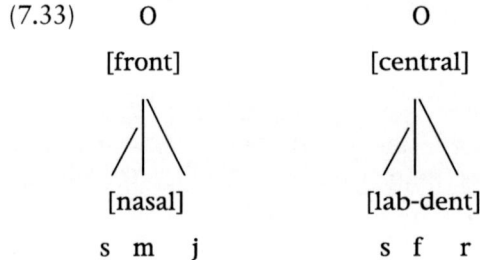

Underspecification of lexical forms enables us to deal with exceptions in this straightforward way.

7.6 VARIATION AND PHONOLOGICAL FORMS

Throughout this book I have tried to determine the balance between phonetics and abstract phonology. Attention to phonetic detail is crucial before we can say for certain what aspects of the speech continuum are important to speakers and hearers. That they may not necessarily be the same for both parties has been pointed out by Cutler (1992), as we saw in section 4.1 above, but nevertheless the debate about the extent of the relevance of phonetic detail continues from various points of view (for example, Archangeli & Pulleyblank, 1994; Johnson & Mullennix, 1997; Local, Ogden & Temple, 2003; Scobbie, 2005a; Silverman, 2006; and the theme of the plenary session of the 16th Manchester Phonology Meeting, as reflected in Cohn, 2008 and Hawkins, 2008).

Silverman (2006: 114–87) discusses three approaches to the way in which phonetic detail might be used in phonological systems: the relaxed constraints model, the prototype model and the exemplar model. All these models assume that phonological categories come from the actual experience a speaker (or group of speakers) has of the utterances around him or her. The relaxed constraints and the prototype models also assume that speakers have some kind of internalized targets for the sounds they hear and produce. In the former case there is a built-in tolerance of (a certain amount of) variation from the targets, a recognition of the nature of the human speech apparatus, which cannot be controlled with the same exact precision on each occasion of use. In the latter case there is an assumption that speakers have exact targets but are incapable of achieving them, so that all instances of utterances are 'mistakes'. Speakers are, by their very nature, inaccurate articulators. But the problem with such an approach is that it does not tell us where the targets come from. How are they acquired? By listening to other, adult inaccurate speakers? The rôle of the prototype seems to be to support, or, perhaps, reflect, the segmental representations of citation forms accepted by most versions of phonology. And in what sense can we justify the notion of inaccuracy in speech, given the very nature of the speech organs? How 'perfect' can the operation of the speech organs be? On the other hand, the exemplar model does not assume some kind of preordained target, but, rather, that the phonological forms develop from within the range of utterances of any particular item a speaker hears. (For a discussion of probability matching in this regard, see Silverman, 2006: 120–54.) Speakers store all instances of utterance in their memory stacks, and the most recent instances that a speaker hears serve as the basis of new utterances. In this way change through one speaker's lifetime can be explained as well as generation-to-generation change. Of course, this process of change and stabilization has to take place within a community of speakers, that is, it must operate for the most part in face-to-face interaction, as was stressed above in section 7.1. If a speaker hears a Bolton accent on the television, she or he will not just pick up that form simply because it is at the top of the memory stack. Usable exemplars must be similar to ones already in the stack and in use. So [fɜː] *fair*, a Lancashire form, will not influence the speech of a Glaswegian, for example. Once again, we need to know what criteria of similarity to apply in such cases, and I have tried to give some answers in this book. I maintain they will mostly be functional criteria and some measure of phonetic similarity based on the phonetic implementation statements of the particular system. Even if speakers do store their experienced utterances in the way the proponents of the exemplar model suggest, there will have to be some kind of phonological form to which these exemplars relate. Otherwise, how do speakers know they are the same linguistic item?

REFERENCES

Anderson, J. M. and C. J. Ewen (1987), *Principles of dependency phonology*. Cambridge: Cambridge University Press.

Archangeli, D. (1984), Underspecification in Yawelmani phonology and morphology. PhD dissertation, MIT.

— (1988), Aspects of underspecification theory. *Phonology* 5: 183–207.

Archangeli, D. and D. Pulleyblank (1994), *Grounded phonology*. Cambridge, MA: MIT Press.

Archangeli, D. and D. T. Langendoen (eds) (1997), *Optimality theory: an overview*. Oxford: Blackwell.

Aronoff, M. and R. Schvaneveldt (1978), Testing morphological productivity. *Annals of the New York Academy of Sciences* 318: 106–14.

Bailey, C. J. (1973), *Variation and linguistic theory*. Washington, DC: Center for Applied Linguistics.

Ball, M. J. (ed.) (1993), *The Celtic languages*. London: Routledge.

Barbour, S. and C. Carmichael (eds) (2000), *Language and nationalism in Europe*. Oxford: Oxford University Press.

Barry, M. C. (1985), A palatographic study of connected speech processes. *Cambridge papers in phonetics and experimental linguistics* 4.

Baudouin de Courtenay, J. [1927] (1972), The difference between phonetics and psychophonetics. Reprinted in E. Stankiewicz (ed.), *A Baudouin de Courtenay reader*. Bloomington: Indiana University Press.

Bendor-Samuel, J. T. (1960), Segmentation in the phonological analysis of Terena. *Word* 16: 348–55. (Also in Palmer, 1970: 214–21.)

Bertelson, P., J. Morais, J. Alegria and A. Content (1985), Phonetic analysis capacity and learning to read. *Nature* 313: 73–4.

Bird, S. (1995), *Computational phonology. A constraint-based approach*. Cambridge: Cambridge University Press.

Bird, S. and E. Klein (1990), Phonological events. *Journal of Linguistics* 26: 33–56.

Blevins, J. (1995), The syllable in phonological theory. In J. A. Goldsmith, *The handbook of phonological theory*.

Bloch, B. and G. L. Trager (1942), *Outline of linguistic analysis*. Baltimore: Linguistic Society of America.

Boase-Beier, J. and K. R. Lodge (2003), *The German language: a linguistic introduction*. Oxford: Blackwell.

Bosch, A. and K. De Jong (1997), The prosody of Barra Gaelic epenthetic vowels. *Studies in the Linguistic Sciences* 27: 2–15.

Brentari, D. (1995), Sign language phonology: ASL. In J. A. Goldsmith, *The handbook of phonological theory*.

Brockhaus, W. (1990), Colourful leagues: a government phonology approach to final obstruent devoicing in German. *UCL Working Papers in Linguistics* 2: 270–97.

Bromberger, S. and M. Halle (1989), Why phonology is different. *Linguistic Inquiry* 20: 51–70.

Bromberger, S. and M. Halle (1997), The contents of phonological signs: a comparison between their use in derivational theories and in optimality theories. In I. Roca, *Derivations and constraints in phonology*.

Carnochan, J. (1957), Gemination in Hausa. In *Studies in Linguistic Analysis*, special volume of the Philological Society: 149–81.

Carr, P. (1993a), *Introduction to phonology*. Basingstoke: MacMillan.

— (1993b), Tongue root harmony, lowness harmony and privative theory. *Newcastle and Durham Working Papers in Linguistics* 1: 42–73.

— (1999), English phonetics and phonology: an introduction. Oxford: Blackwell.

Carter, P. (2003), Extrinsic phonetic interpretation: spectral variation in English liquids. In Local, Ogden and Temple, *Phonetic Interpretation*.

Carter, P. and J. K. Local (2007), F2 variation in Newcastle and Leeds English liquid systems. *Journal of the International Phonetic Association* 37: 183–99.

Charette, M. (1991), *Conditions on phonological government*. Cambridge: Cambridge University Press.

Chomsky, A. N. (1964), *Current issues in linguistic theory*. The Hague: Mouton.

— (1980), *Rules and representations*. Oxford: Blackwell.

Chomsky, A. N. and M. Halle (1968), *The sound pattern of English*. New York: Harper and Row.

Clark, J. and C. Yallop (1995), *An introduction to phonetics and phonology* (2nd edn). Oxford: Blackwell.

Clements, G. N. (1992), Comments on Ohala's paper (chapter 7). In G. J. Docherty and D. R. Ladd, *Papers in laboratory phonology II*.

Clements, G. N. and E. Hume (1995), The internal organization of speech sounds. In J. A. Goldsmith, *The handbook of phonological theory*.

Cohn, A. (2008), The nature of lexical representation: fine-grained *and* abstract. Paper presented to the 16th Manchester Phonology Meeting, May, 2008.

Cole, J. and L. Trigo (1988), Parasitic harmony. In H. van der Hulst and N. Smith (eds), *Features, segmental structure and harmony processes II*. Dordrecht: Foris: 19–38.

Coleman, J. (1995), Declarative lexical phonology. In J. Durand and F. Katamba, *Frontiers of phonology.*

Cutler, A. (1992), Psychology and the segment. In G. J. Docherty and D. R. Ladd, *Papers in laboratory phonology II.*

Davenport, M. and S. J. Hannahs (2005), *Introducing phonetics and phonology* (2nd edn). London: Hodder Arnold.

Dilworth, A. and M. Macleod (no date), *A structural approach to learning Scottish Gaelic; Part 1 – Phonetics and speech training.* Fort Augustus: The Abbey Press. (c.1980)

Docherty, G. J. and P. Foulkes (2000), Speaker, speech and knowledge of sounds. In N. Burton-Roberts, P. Carr and G. J. Docherty (eds), *Phonological knowledge.* Oxford: Oxford University Press: 161–84.

Docherty, G. J. and D. R. Ladd (eds) (1992), *Papers in laboratory phonology II.* Cambridge: Cambridge University Press.

Dorian, N. C. (1965), A phonological description of Brora, Golspie and Embo Gaelic: an East Sutherland dialect. PhD dissertation, University of Michigan.

— (1977), A hierarchy of morphophonemic decay in Scottish Gaelic language death: the differential failure of lenition. *Word* 28: 96–109.

— (1982), Defining the speech community to include its working margins. In S. Romaine (ed.), *Sociolinguistic variation in speech communities.* London: Edward Arnold: 25–33.

Durand, J. (2005), Tense/lax, the vowel system of English and phonological theory. In P. Carr, J. Durand and C. J. Ewen (eds), *Headhood, elements, specification and contrastivity.* Amsterdam: John Benjamins: 77–97.

Durand, J. and F. Katamba (eds) (1995), *Frontiers of phonology: primitives, architectures and derivation.* London: Longman.

Evans, N. (1995), Current issues in the phonology of Australian languages. In J. A. Goldsmith, *The handbook of phonological theory.*

Fasold, R. (1984), *The sociolinguistics of society.* Oxford: Blackwell.

Ferguson, C. A. (1978), Phonological processes. In J. H. Greenberg (ed.) *Universals of human language. Volume 2 Phonology.* Stanford: Stanford University Press: 403–42.

Firth, J. R. (1935), Phonological features of some Indian languages. Reprinted in Firth (1957): 47–53.

— (1948), Sounds and prosodies. *Transactions of the Philological Society*: 127–52. (Also in Palmer, 1970: 1–26.)

— (1957), *Papers in linguistics.* London: Oxford University Press.

Fischer, O. (1992), Syntax. In N. Blake (ed.), *The Cambridge history of the English language Volume II: 1066–1476.* Cambridge: Cambridge University Press: 207–408.

Fourakis, M. and R. Port (1986), Stop epenthesis in English. *Journal of Phonetics* 14: 197–221.

Fox, A. (1990), *The structure of German.* Oxford: Oxford University Press.

Fudge, E. C. (1967), On the nature of phonological primes. *Journal of Linguistics* 3: 1–36.

— (1969), Syllables. *Journal of Linguistics* 5: 253–87.

Giegerich, H. (1985), *Metrical structure and metrical phonology: German and English*. Cambridge: Cambridge University Press.

— (1986), *A relational model of German syllable structure*. Duisburg: L.A.U.D.T.

— (1992), *English phonology*. Cambridge: Cambridge University Press.

Gillies, W. (1993), Scottish Gaelic. In Ball, *The Celtic languages*.

Gimson, A. C. (1962), *An introduction to the pronunciation of English*. London: Edward Arnold.

Goldsmith, J. A. (1990), *Autosegmental and metrical phonology*. Oxford: Basil Blackwell.

— (ed.) (1995a), *The handbook of phonological theory*. Oxford: Blackwell.

— (1995b), Phonological theory. In J. A. Goldsmith, *The handbook of phonological theory*.

Griffen, T. D. (1985), *Aspects of dynamic phonology*. Amsterdam: John Benjamins.

Grinter, R. (2005), *The quantum in chemistry: an experimentalist's view*. Chichester: John Wiley and Sons.

Gussenhoven, C. and H. Jacobs (2005), *Understanding phonology* (2nd edn). London: Arnold.

Gussmann, E. (2002), *Phonology*. Cambridge: Cambridge University Press.

Hale, M. and C. Reiss (2000), Phonology as cognition. In N. Burton-Roberts, P. Carr and G. J. Docherty (eds), *Phonological knowledge*. Oxford: Oxford University Press: 161–84.

Hall, B. L., R. M. R. Hall, M. D. Pam, A. Myers, S. A. Antell and G. K. Cherono (1974), African vowel harmony from the vantage point of Kalenjin. *Afrika und Übersee* LVII: 241–67.

Hall, N. (2006), Cross-linguistic patterns of vowel intrusion. *Phonology* 23: 387–429.

Halle, M. and J-R. Vergnaud (1981), Harmony processes. In W. Klein and W. Levelt (eds), *Crossing the boundaries in linguistics*. Dordrecht: Reidel: 1–22.

Harris, J. (1994), *English sound structure*. Oxford: Blackwell.

Harris, J. and G. Lindsey (1995), The elements of phonological representation. In J. Durand and F. Katamba, *Frontiers of phonology*.

Hawkins, S. (2008), Contributions of phonetic detail to the mental lexicon. Paper presented to the 16th Manchester Phonology Meeting, May, 2008.

Heggarty, P. (2000), Quantifying change over time in phonetics. In C. Renfrew, A. McMahon and L. Trask (eds), *Time depth in historical linguistics*. Cambridge: McDonald Institute for Archaeological Research: 531–61.

Heggarty, P. and A. McMahon (2002), How similar are sounds? Paper presented to the 10th Manchester Phonology Meeting, May, 2002.

Helgason, P. (2002), Preaspiration in the Nordic languages: synchronic and diachronic aspects. PhD dissertation, University of Stockholm.

Hockett, C. F. (1954), Two models of grammatical description. *Word* 10: 210–34.

— (1955), *A manual of phonology*. International Journal of American Linguistics Memoir 11. Baltimore: Waverly Press Inc.

Honikman, B. (1964), Articulatory settings. In D. Abercrombie, D. B. Fry, P. A. D. MacCarthy, N. C. Scott and J. L. M. Trim (eds), *In honour of Daniel Jones*. London: Longmans Green: 73–84.

Houston, A. (1985), Continuity and change in English morphology: the variable (ING). PhD dissertation, University of Pennsylvania.

Hulst, H. van der and J. van de Weijer (1995), Vowel harmony. In J. A. Goldsmith, *The handbook of phonological theory*.

Itô, J. and R. A. Mester (1995), Japanese phonology. In J. A. Goldsmith, *The handbook of phonological theory*.

Iverson, G. K. (1995), Rule ordering. In J. A. Goldsmith, *The handbook of phonological theory*.

Jaeger, J. J. (1986), On the acquisition of abstract representations for English vowels. *Phonology Yearbook* 3: 71–97.

Jakobson, R., C. G. M. Fant and M. Halle (1951), *Preliminaries to speech analysis*. Cambridge, MA: MIT Press.

Jakobson, R. and M. Halle (1964), Tenseness and laxness. In D. Abercrombie, D. B. Fry, P. A. D. MacCarthy, N. C. Scott and J. L. M. Trim (eds), *In honour of Daniel Jones*. London: Longmans Green: 96–101.

Johnson, K. and J. W. Mullenix (eds) (1997), *Talker variability in speech processing*. New York: Academic Press.

Jones, M. J. (2002), The origin of Definite Article Reduction in northern dialects: evidence from dialect allomorphy. *English Language and Linguistics* 6: 325–45.

— (2007), Glottals and grammar: Definite Article Reduction and morpheme boundaries. *Leeds Working Papers in Linguistics* 12: 61–77.

Kager, R. (1999), *Optimality theory*. Cambridge: Cambridge University Press.

Kahn, D. (1976), Syllable-based generalizations in English phonology. PhD dissertation, MIT.

Kaisse, E. and P. A. Shaw (1985), On the theory of lexical phonology. *Phonology Yearbook* 2: 1–30.

Kaye, J., J. Lowenstamm and J-R. Vergnaud (1985), The internal structure of phonological elements: a theory of charm and government. *Phonology Yearbook* 2: 305–28.

Keating, P. A. (1988), Underspecification in phonetics. *Phonology* 5: 275–92.

Kelly, J. and J. K. Local (1986), Long-domain resonance patterns in English. In *International conference on speech input/output; techniques and applications*. Conference publication no. 258. London: IEE: 304–9.

Kelly, J. and J. K. Local (1989), *Doing phonology*. Manchester: Manchester University Press.

Kenstowicz, M. (1994), *Phonology in generative grammar*. Oxford: Blackwell.

Kerswill, P. (1985), A sociophonetic study of connected speech processes in Cambridge English: an outline and some results. *Cambridge papers in phonetics and experimental linguistics* 4.

Kessler, B. (2005), Phonetic comparison algorithms. *Transactions of the Philological Society* 103: 243–60.

Kingsley O'Hagan, V. and M. Krämer (2004), The realization of Irish initial consonant mutations by L2 learners and the universal markedness hierarchy of place features. Paper presented to the 12th Manchester Phonology Meeting, Manchester, May 2004.

Kohler, K. J. (1977), *Einführung in die Phonetik des Deutschen*. Berlin: Erich Schmidt.

Krämer, M. (2008), Taking a free ride can cau[ɹ]se severe hyperrhoticity. Paper presented to the 16th Manchester Phonology Meeting, May, 2008.

Kruszewski, M. [1883] (1995), An outline of linguistic science. Reprinted in K. Koerner (ed.), *Writings in general linguistics*. Amsterdam: John Benjamins.

Labov, W. (1966), *The social stratification of English in New York City*. Washington, DC: Center for Applied Linguistics.

— (1972), *Sociolinguistic patterns*. Philadelphia: University of Pennsylvania Press.

Ladefoged, P. (1968), *A phonetic study of West African languages* (2nd edn). Cambridge: Cambridge University Press.

— (1971), *Preliminaries to linguistic phonetics*. Chicago: University of Chicago Press.

— (1972), Phonological features and their phonetic correlates. *Journal of the International Phonetic Association* 2: 2–12.

— (1982), *A course in phonetics* (2nd edn). New York: Harcourt, Brace and Jovanovich.

— (2003), Commentary: some thoughts on syllables – an old-fashioned interlude. In J. K. Local, Ogden and Temple, *Phonetic interpretation*.

Lass, R. (1976), *English phonology and phonological theory*. Cambridge: Cambridge University Press.

— (1984), *Phonology*. Cambridge: Cambridge University Press.

— (1992), Phonology and morphology. In N. Blake (ed.), *The Cambridge history of the English language Volume II: 1066–1476*. Cambridge: Cambridge University Press: 23–155.

Levergood, B. (1984), Rule governed vowel harmony and the strict cycle. *Proceedings of NELS* 14: 275–93.

Lindau, M. E. (1975), Features for vowels. *UCLA Working Papers in Phonetics* 30.

— (1978), Vowel features. *Language* 54: 541–63.

Lindau, M., L. Jacobson and P. Ladefoged (1973), The feature advanced tongue root. *UCLA Working Papers in Phonetics* 22: 76–94.

Local, J. K. (1992), Modelling assimilation in non-segmental rule-free synthesis. In G. J. Docherty, G. and D.R. Ladd, *Papers in laboratory phonology II*.

Local, J. K. and K. R. Lodge (1996), Another Travesty of Representation: phonological representation and phonetic interpretation of ATR harmony in Kalenjin. *York Papers in Linguistics* 17: 77–117.

— (2004), Some auditory and acoustic observations on the phonetics of [ATR] harmony in a speaker of a dialect of Kalenjin. *Journal of the International Phonetic Association* 34: 1–16.

Local, J. K., R. A. Ogden and R. Temple (eds) (2003), *Phonetic interpretation: papers in laboratory phonology VI*. Cambridge: Cambridge University Press.

Lodge, K. R. (1971), The German strong verbs: a prosodic statement. *Archivum Linguisticum* [new series] 2: 71–94.

— (1973), Stockport revisited. *Journal of the International Phonetic Association* 3: 81–7.

— (1983), The acquisition of phonology: a Stockport sample. *Lingua* 61: 335–51.

— (1984), *Studies in the phonology of colloquial English*. London: Croom Helm.

— (1986), The English velar fricative, dialect variation and dependency phonology. In J. Durand (ed.), *Dependency and non-linear phonology*. London: Croom Helm.

— (1987), What the L R liquids? A problem for concrete phonologies. Paper presented to the Linguistics Association of Great Britain, Bradford.

— (1989), A non-segmental account of German Umlaut: diachronic and synchronic perspectives. *Linguistische Berichte* 124: 470–91.

— (1991/2003), *The standard English pattern*. Norwich: private publication.

— (1992), Assimilation, deletion paths and underspecification. *Journal of Linguistics* 28: 13–52.

— (1993), Underspecification, polysystemicity and non-segmental representations in phonology: an analysis of Malay. *Linguistics* 31: 475–519.

— (1995), Kalenjin phonology and morphology: a further exemplification of underspecification and non-destructive phonology. *Lingua* 96: 29–43.

— (1997), Some handy notes on phonology. *Journal of Linguistics* 33: 153–69.

— (2001), The modern reflexes of some Middle English vowel contrasts in Norfolk and Norwich. In J. Fisiak and P. J. Trudgill (eds), *East Anglian English*. Cambridge: D. S. Brewer: 205–15.

— (2003a), A declarative treatment of the phonetics and phonology of German rhymal /r/. *Lingua* 113: 931–51.

— (2003b), Phonological translation and phonetic repertoire. *International Journal of Applied Linguistics* 13: 263–76.

— (2005), Representation and the rôle of underspecification in declarative phonology. In P. Carr, J. Durand and C. J. Ewen (eds), *Headhood, elements, specification and contrastivity*. Amsterdam: John Benjamins: 235–54.

— (2007), Timing, segmental status and aspiration in Icelandic. *Transactions of the Philological Society* 105: 66–104.

— (2009), *A critical introduction to phonetics*. London: Continuum.

Lodge, K. R., J. K. Local and S. Harlow (in prep), Intrinsic phonetic interpretation and the problems of ATR harmony and its domains in Tugen.

MacAulay, D. (ed.) (1992), *The Celtic languages*. Cambridge: Cambridge University Press.

Macdonald, D. (ed.) (2001), *The new encyclopaedia of mammals*. Oxford: Oxford University Press.

Macken, M. A. (1995), Phonological acquisition. In J. A. Goldsmith, *The handbook of phonological theory*.

Mann, V. A. (1986), Phonological awareness: the role of reading experience. *Cognition* 24: 65–92.

Martinez-Celdrán, E. (2004), Problems in the classification of approximants. *Journal of the International Phonetic Association* 34: 201–10.

Mohanan, K. P. (1995), The organization of the grammar. In J. A. Goldsmith, *The handbook of phonological theory*.

Morais, J. (1991), Phonological awareness: a bridge between language and literacy. In D. J. Sawyer and B. J. Fox (eds), *Phonological awareness in reading: the evolution of current perspectives*. Berlin: Springer-Verlag: 31–71.

Morais, J., P. Bertelson, L. Cary and J. Alegria (1986), Literacy training and speech segmentation. *Cognition* 24: 45–64.

Morais, J., L. Cary, J. Alegria and P. Bertelson (1979), Does awareness of speech as a sequence of phones arise spontaneously? *Cognition* 7: 323–31.

Newton, B. (1970), *Cypriot Greek, its phonology and inflections*. The Hague: Mouton.

Nolan, F. (1992), The descriptive role of segments: evidence from assimilation. In G. J. Docherty and D. R. Ladd, *Papers in laboratory phonology II*.

Nolan, F., T. Holst and B. Kühnert (1996), Modelling [s] to [ʃ] accommodation in English. *Journal of Phonetics* 24: 113–37.

Odden, D. (2005), *Introducing phonology*. Cambridge: Cambridge University Press.

Ogden, R. A. (1997), "It's" unusual. Paper presented to the Fifth Manchester Phonology Meeting, May, 1997.

— (1999), A declarative account of strong and weak auxiliaries in English. *Phonology* 16: 55–92.

Orton, H. et al. (1962–71), *Survey of English dialects, volumes I – IV*. Leeds: E. J. Arnold.

Palmer, F. R. (ed.) (1970), *Prosodic analysis*. London: Oxford University Press.

Paradis, C. and J-F. Prunet (eds) (1991), *The special status of coronals* (Vol. 2 of *Phonetics and Phonology*). San Diego: Academic Press.

Paul, H. [1890] (1970), *Principles of the history of language*. College Park: McGrath.

Petyt, K. M. (1980), *The study of dialect*. London: André Deutsch.

Pierrehumbert, J. (1990), Phonological and phonetic representation. *Journal of Phonetics* 18: 375–94.

Pike, K. L. (1947), *Phonemics*. Ann Arbor: University of Michigan Press.

Plug, L. and R. Ogden (2003), A parametric approach to the phonetics of postvocalic /r/ in Dutch. *Phonetica* 60: 159–86.

Pulleyblank, D. (1988a), Vocalic underspecification in Yoruba. *Linguistic Inquiry* 19: 233–70.

— (1988b), Underspecification, the feature hierarchy and Tiv vowels. *Phonology* 5: 299–326.

— (1997), Optimality Theory and features. In D. Archangeli and D. T. Langendoen, *Optimality theory*.

Read, C., Z. Yun-Fei, N. Hong-Yin and D. Bao-Qing (1986), The ability to manipulate speech sounds depends on knowing alphabetic writing. *Cognition* 24: 31–44.

Ringen, C. (1988), Underspecification theory and binary features. In H. van der Hulst and N. Smith (eds), *Features, segmental structure and harmony processes (Part II)*. Dordrecht: Foris: 145–60.

— (1999), Aspiration, preaspiration, deaspiration, sonorant devoicing and spirantization in Icelandic. *Nordic Journal of Linguistics* 22: 137–56.

Ringen, C. and P. Helgason (2004), Distinctive [voice] does not imply regressive assimilation: evidence from Swedish. *International Journal of English Studies* 4: 53–71.

Robins, R. H. (1953), The phonology of the nasalized verbal forms in Sundanese. *Bulletin of the School of Oriental and African Studies* 15: 138–45. (Also in Palmer, 1970: 104–11.)

Roca, I. (ed.) (1997), *Derivations and constraints in phonology*. Oxford: Oxford University Press.

Romaine, S. (1982), What is a speech community? In S. Romaine (ed.)

Sociolinguistic variation in speech communities. London: Edward Arnold: 13–24.

Rupp, L. and H. Page-Verhoeff (2005), Pragmatic and historical aspects of Definite Article Reduction in northern English dialects. *English World-Wide* 26: 325–46.

Russell, P. (1995), *An introduction to the Celtic languages*. London: Longman.

Sadie, S. and J. Tyrrell (2001), *The new Grove dictionary of music*. 2nd edn. London: Macmillan.

Schane, S. A. (1968), *French phonology and morphology*. Cambridge, MA: MIT Press.

— (1973), *Generative phonology*. Englewood Cliffs, NJ: Prentice-Hall.

Scobbie, J. M. (1997), *Autosegmental representation in a declarative constraint-based framework*. New York: Garland.

— (2005a), The phonetics–phonology overlap. *Working Paper WP-1*. Edinburgh: Queen Margaret University College.

— (2005b), Interspeaker variation among Shetland Islanders as the long term outcome of dialectally varied input: speech production evidence for fine-grained linguistic plasticity. *Working Paper WP-2*. Edinburgh: Queen Margaret University College.

Scobbie, J. M., S. Bird and J. Coleman (1996), Key aspects of declarative phonology. In J. Durand and B. Laks (eds), *Current trends in phonology*. Salford: ESRI: 685–710.

Selkirk, E. O. (1982), Syllables. In H. van der Hulst and N. Smith (eds), *The structure of phonological representations (Vol. II)*. Dordrecht: Foris: 337–83.

— (1984), On the major class features and syllable theory. In M. Aronoff and R. T. Oerhle (eds), *Language sound structure*. Cambridge, MA: MIT Press: 107–36.

Shepard, R., C. Hovland and H. Jenkins (1961), Learning and memorizing of classifications. *Psychological Monographs* 75(13): Whole No. 517.

Silverman, D. (2006), *A critical introduction to phonology: of sound, mind and body*. London: Continuum.

Simpson, A. P. (1998), Accounting for the phonetics of German *r* without processes. *ZAS Papers in Linguistics* 11: 91–104.

Smith, N. V. (1973), *The acquisition of phonology*. Cambridge: Cambridge University Press.

Spencer, A. (1996), *Phonology*. Oxford: Blackwell.

Sprigg, K. (1957), Junction in spoken Burmese. *Studies in Linguistic Analysis* 104–38.

SILA (1957), *Studies in linguistic analysis*. Special volume of the Philological Society.

Stemberger, J. P. (1991), Radical underspecification in language production. *Phonology* 8: 73–112.

Steriade, D. (1995), Underspecification and markedness. In J. A. Goldsmith, *The handbook of phonological theory.*

Stewart, J. M. (1967), Tongue root position in Akan vowel harmony. *Phonetica* 16: 185–204.

Ternes, E. (1989), *The phonemic analysis of Scots Gaelic.* 2nd edn. Hamburg: Helmut Buske Verlag.

Trubetzkoy, N. S. (1936), Die Aufhebung der phonologischen Gegensätze. *TCLP* VI: 29–45.

— (1939), *Grundzüge der Phonologie.* Göttingen: Vandenhoek and Ruprecht.

Trudgill, P. J. (1974), *The social differentiation of English in Norwich.* Cambridge: Cambridge University Press.

— (1983), *On dialect.* Oxford: Basil Blackwell.

— (1986), *Dialects in contact.* Oxford: Basil Blackwell.

Trudgill, P. J. and T. Foxcroft (1978), On the sociolinguistics of vocalic mergers: transfer and approximation in East Anglia. In P. J. Trudgill (ed.), *Sociolinguistic patterns in British English.* London: Edward Arnold: 69–79.

Tsujimura, N. (1996), *An introduction to Japanese linguistics.* Oxford: Blackwell.

Tucker, A. N. and M. A. Mpaayei (1955), *Linguistic analyses: the non-Bantu languages of North-Eastern Africa.* London: Oxford University Press.

Vanvik, A. (1979), *Norsk fonetikk.* Oslo: University of Oslo.

Wang, H. S. and B. L. Derwing (1986), More on English vowel shift: the back vowel question. *Phonology Yearbook* 3: 99–116.

Warrington, J. (ed.) (1956), *The Paston letters.* London: Dent.

Waterson, N. (1956), Some aspects of the phonology of the nominal forms of the Turkish word. *Bulletin of the School of Oriental and African Studies* 18: 578–91. (Also in Palmer 1970: 174–87.)

— (1987), *Prosodic phonology: the theory and its application to language acquisition and speech processing.* Newcastle upon Tyne: Grevatt and Grevatt.

Wells, J. C. (1982), *Accents of English.* 3 vols, Cambridge: Cambridge University Press.

West, P. (1997), The extent of secondary articulations. Paper presented to the Fifth Manchester Phonology Meeting, Manchester, May 1997.

— (1999), Perception of distributed coarticulatory properties of English /l/ and /ɹ/. *Journal of Phonetics* 27: 405–26.

Wiese, R. (1996), *The phonology of German.* Oxford: Oxford University Press.

Wright, S. (1986), The interaction of sociolinguistic and phonetically-conditioned CSPS in Cambridge English: auditory and electropalatographic evidence. *Cambridge papers in phonetics and experimental linguistics* 5.

INDEX